D0080707

Do Not Discard!

This is your Registration Key for FinGame Online 5.0.

TO REGISTER:

1. Go to: http://www.mhhe.com/fingame5

2. Select the "Click Here to Activate a New Account" button.

3. Enter your Registration Key, printed below, in the "New account registration" frame that appears and select the "Activate a new account" button.

RPEF-MSBW-GTCT-JEBB-VVFF

4. You will then be prompted to enter required account information including a unique User Name and Password.

5. Your new account will be activated.

6. You will need to enter a group code provided by your instructor before you can access all of the features in the game and participate with your class.

This code will give you 6 months of access to FinGame Online 5.0. If you purchased a used book, this code has expired or soon will expire.

ISBN 978-0-07-721729-7
MHID 0-07-721729-2

FinGame Online 5.0

The Financial Management Decision Game
Participant's Manual

The McGraw-Hill/Irwin Series in Finance, Insurance and Real Estate

Stephen A. Ross
Franco Modigliani Professor of Finance and Economics
Sloan School of Management
Massachusetts Institute of Technology
Consulting Editor

FINANCIAL MANAGEMENT

Adair
Excel Applications for Corporate Finance
First Edition

Benninga and Sarig
Corporate Finance: *A Valuation Approach*

Block and Hirt
Foundations of Financial Management
Twelfth Edition

Brealey, Myers, and Allen
Principles of Corporate Finance
Eighth Edition

Brealey, Myers, and Marcus
Fundamentals of Corporate Finance
Fifth Edition

Brooks
FinGame Online 5.0

Bruner
Case Studies in Finance: *Managing for Corporate Value Creation*
Fifth Edition

Chew
The New Corporate Finance: *Where Theory Meets Practice*
Third Edition

Chew and Gillan
Corporate Governance at the Crossroads: *A Book of Readings*
First Edition

DeMello
Cases in Finance
Second Edition

Grinblatt (editor)
Stephen A. Ross, Mentor: *Influence Through Generations*

Grinblatt and Titman
Financial Markets and Corporate Strategy
Second Edition

Helfert
Techniques of Financial Analysis: *A Guide to Value Creation*
Eleventh Edition

Higgins
Analysis for Financial Management
Eighth Edition

Kester, Ruback, and Tufano
Case Problems in Finance
Twelfth Edition

Ross, Westerfield, and Jaffe
Corporate Finance
Eighth Edition

Ross, Westerfield, Jaffe, and Jordan
Corporate Finance: *Core Principles and Applications*
First Edition

Ross, Westerfield, and Jordan
Essentials of Corporate Finance
Fifth Edition

Ross, Westerfield, and Jordan
Fundamentals of Corporate Finance
Eighth Edition

Shefrin
Behavioral Corporate Finance: *Decisions that Create Value*
First Edition

White
Financial Analysis with an Electronic Calculator
Sixth Edition

INVESTMENTS

Adair
Excel Applications for Investments
First Edition

Bodie, Kane, and Marcus
Essentials of Investments
Sixth Edition

Bodie, Kane, and Marcus
Investments
Seventh Edition

Hirt and Block
Fundamentals of Investment Management
Eighth Edition

Hirschey and Nofsinger
Investments: *Analysis and Behavior*
First Edition

Jordan and Miller
Fundamentals of Investments: *Valuation and Management*
Fourth Edition

FINANCIAL INSTITUTIONS AND MARKETS

Rose and Hudgins
Bank Management and Financial Services
Seventh Edition

Rose and Marquis
Money and Capital Markets: *Financial Institutions and Instruments in a Global Marketplace*
Ninth Edition

Saunders and Cornett
Financial Institutions Management: *A Risk Management Approach*
Fifth Edition

Saunders and Cornett
Financial Markets and Institutions: *An Introduction to the Risk Management Approach*
Third Edition

INTERNATIONAL FINANCE

Eun and Resnick
International Financial Management
Fourth Edition

Kuemmerle
Case Studies in International Entrepreneurship: *Managing and Financing Ventures in the Global Economy*
First Edition

REAL ESTATE

Brueggeman and Fisher
Real Estate Finance and Investments
Thirteenth Edition

Corgel, Ling, and Smith
Real Estate Perspectives: *An Introduction to Real Estate*
Fourth Edition

Ling and Archer
Real Estate Principles: *A Value Approach*
Second Edition

FINANCIAL PLANNING AND INSURANCE

Allen, Melone, Rosenbloom, and Mahoney
Retirement Plans: *401(k)s, IRAs, and Other Deferred Compensation Approaches*
Tenth Edition

Altfest
Personal Financial Planning
First Edition

Harrington and Niehaus
Risk Management and Insurance
Second Edition

Kapoor, Dlabay, and Hughes
Focus on Personal Finance: *An Active Approach to Help You Develop Successful Financial Skills*
First Edition

Kapoor, Dlabay, and Hughes
Personal Finance
Eighth Edition

FinGame Online 5.0

The Financial Management Decision Game
Participant's Manual

LeRoy D. Brooks

John Carroll University

David W. Brooks

Programmer

Boston   Burr Ridge, IL   Dubuque, IA   Madison, WI   New York   San Francisco   St. Louis
Bangkok   Bogotá   Caracas   Kuala Lumpur   Lisbon   London   Madrid   Mexico City
Milan   Montreal   New Delhi   Santiago   Seoul   Singapore   Sydney   Taipei   Toronto

McGraw-Hill
Irwin

FINGAME ONLINE 5.0 PARTICIPANT'S MANUAL
Published by McGraw-Hill/Irwin, a business unit of The McGraw-Hill Companies, Inc., 1221 Avenue of the Americas, New York, NY, 10020. Copyright © 2008 by The McGraw-Hill Companies, Inc. All rights reserved. No part of this publication may be reproduced or distributed in any form or by any means, or stored in a database or retrieval system, without the prior written consent of The McGraw-Hill Companies, Inc., including, but not limited to, in any network or other electronic storage or transmission, or broadcast for distance learning.

Some ancillaries, including electronic and print components, may not be available to customers outside the United States.

This book is printed on acid-free paper.

Printed in the United States of America.

12 13 14 15 16 QVS/ 22 21 20 19

ISBN   978-0-07-331355-9
MHID   0-07-331355-6

Executive editor: *Michele Janicek*
Editorial assistant: *Katherine Mau*
Senior marketing manager: *Julie Phifer*
Project manager: *Kathryn D. Mikulic*
Senior production supervisor: *Carol A. Bielski*
Senior designer: *Kami Carter*
Cover image: *Digital Vision*
Typeface: *11/13 Times Roman*
Compositor: *ICC Macmillan Inc.*
Printer: *Quad/Graphics*

Library of Congress Cataloging-in-Publication Data

Brooks, LeRoy D.
    FinGame online 5.0 : the financial management decision game participant's manual/LeRoy
D. Brooks. — 5th ed.
        p. cm. — (The McGraw-Hill/Irwin series in finance, insurance, and real estate)
    Rev. ed. of: FinGame online 4.0. 4th ed. 2000.
    Includes index.
    ISBN-13: 978-0-07-331355-9 (alk. paper)
    ISBN-10: 0-07-331355-6 (alk. paper)
    1. Corporations—Finance—Computer games. 2. Management games—Computer programs.
I. Brooks, LeRoy D. FinGame online 4.0. II. Title.
HG4012.5.B757 2008
658.150285'53—dc22

                                                                                    2007018495

www.mhhe.com

Preface

FinGame Online 5.0: The Financial Management Decision Game is a comprehensive multiple-period finance case. The game helps the student develop and enhance skills in financial management, financial accounting statement analysis, and general decision making. FinGame operates on the McGraw-Hill Internet site, enabling Web access worldwide.

The multiple-period decision-making setting provided in FinGame cannot be duplicated with standard cases or problems. In the game, feedback on the results of prior decisions is received every period of play. Good or bad decisions immediately impact the company's performance and its relative position to other companies. Like the real world, and not like standard cases, the good or bad decisions in the game generally have long-term continuing consequences that plague the firm with the poor decision and strengthen the firm with the better decision. This positive and negative reinforcement throughout the game promotes learning of financial definitions, analytic tools, and appropriate solution techniques.

A multiple-period environment also forces students to recognize the importance of maintaining future flexibility in making decisions. Flexibility is retained by avoiding decisions that eliminate a large set of feasible future company decision options. With single-stage problems, the consequences of the future restrictions caused by a given decision are usually never recognized, and clearly never experienced. Static single-period cases and models fail to adequately capture the complexities of an actual environment.

The manager's and company's long-term prosperity and competitiveness come from a planned effort to control the breadth of the future set of available decisions through the manager's current decisions. FinGame provides this experience.

The primary focus of the game is directed toward finance. Participants in the game control the major financial decision areas of a company. The decisions include both the internal management of the firm and the external acquisition of assets and financing. The FinGame company managers have approximately the same degree of control as actual companies in paying dividends; issuing or retiring preferred and common stock; and issuing, retiring, and refunding several different types of debt. Additionally, decisions are required on short-term investments, the risk level of short-term investments, sales discounts, capital budgeting projects, and various production decisions that affect the finance function.

This fairly complex company environment enables students to gain insights into the interrelationships among financing, capital budgeting, liquidity management, accounting, production, and capacity management. Few constraints are placed on the set of decisions in the game that are not found in actual companies. This makes the game more realistic.

Yet, to better enable student learning, the number of decision options found in actual companies is purposely not available in the game. Too many decisions that have interactions with each other become much more difficult to evaluate and manage successfully. With greater experience and more complex decision models, students can successfully tackle the more difficult ones when their experience and monetary rewards are far greater. As an analogy, a child has to learn to crawl before she can walk and walk before she can run. Our hope in FinGame is to get the participant from the equivalent of the crawling stage to at least the walking part, even if then a bit shaky.

FG provides a simulation requiring the application of theory, analytical tools, and solution procedures that must be learned outside the game. The game and manual are supplements to be used with standard texts; they are not replacements for texts. In this context, the game is a dynamic multiple-period case that provides the student with many different types of problems requiring solution.

Acknowledgments

Most credit for the current edition clearly belongs to my friend and son, David W. Brooks. New editions would not be possible without his extensive contributions. David has provided tremendous time, dedication, and knowledge to creating the programming for this version and creating the new Web interface.

Many others have contributed to the prior game development and this current version, and they deserve special thanks. I thank the many students who have provided valuable suggestions and comments. I am especially appreciative of the instructors who have uncovered underlying "bugs" and problems while also providing suggestions for improving the game. Very helpful comments leading to changes since the last edition, and changes that will occur in the future, came from Professors John Bilson, Robert J. Boldin, Robert Burney, Gary Caton, Paul Haensly, Thomas Hardy, Brian Holland, Niles Logue, David Martin, Christine McClatchey, William Nelson, Carolyn Spencer, Inchul Suh, Theodore Veit, Penny Wrightman, Thomas Willey, Arthur Wilson, and Tong Yao. Any errors that remain are David's and my responsibility.

LeRoy D. Brooks

Contents

1 Introduction   1

Overview   1
The Purpose of the Game   2
Text Contents   2
The Game Environment   3
Preparation Requirements   7

2 Web Access and Use   9

Overview   9
Computer Requirements   9
Initial Instructions   10
Getting a Company Account   11
Operating a FinGame Company   11
Details on Main Menu Options   13
  Basic Account Information   13
  Change User Name   13
  Change Password   13
  Enabling Other Unique FG Features   13
Process for Quarterly Company Simulations   14
  Edit Pro Forma Decision Inputs   14
  Edit Actual Decision Inputs   16
  Run Actual Simulation   16
The Underlying Simulation   16

3 Establishing a Management Plan   19

Overview   19
  Accumulated Wealth   19
  How Is Accumulated Wealth Maximized?   20
The Need for a Company Strategy   20
A Plan of Attack in FinGame Online   21
  A Possible Planning Approach   22
  The Need for Pro Forma Statements   22
  Cash and Liquidity Management   23
  Capital Budgeting Analysis   24
  Capital Structure and Weighted Average Cost of Capital   25

Dividend Policy   27
Discount on Receivables   28
Production Strategy   29
Unit Pricing Strategy   30
Advertising   34
Integrating the Set of Decisions   35
Company Life Cycle   37
New Companies   37
Mature and Declining Companies   38
Life Cycle Impacts on Overall Strategy   38
Managers' Risk-Bearing Tolerance   39
Risk Bearing in Actual Companies   39
Managers' Risk Tolerance in FinGame   40
Conclusion   41

4   The Company Environment and Rules   43

Overview   43
Company Management Instructions   43
Company Operating Rules   45
The Industry Environment   45
Operation of the Company   46
Revenues   47
Product Sales Estimation   47
Purchase of Demand and Price Forecast   49
Product Demanded and Sold   50
Manager Control of Product Pricing   51
Sales Discounts   51
Cash Management   52
Short-Term Investments   52
Risk Level of Short-Term Investments   53
Cash Shortages and Marketable Securities Liquidation   53
Cash Shortages and Short-Term Penalty Loans   54
Production Costs   55
Materials   56
Direct Labor   56
Warehouse Fees   57
Plant   57
Machinery   58
Capital Budgeting Projects   60
Other Overhead   62
Summary on Production Costs   63
Selling and Administrative Expenses   63
Advertising Costs   64
Extraordinary Items   64
Labor Strike   64
Extraordinary Loss or Gain   65
Fire   65
Loans and Debt Costs   66
Short-Term Loans   67
Short-Term Penalty Loans   68
Intermediate-Term Loans   68
Long-Term Bonds   70
Taxes   71

Equities   72
   Preferred Stock   72
   Common Stock   75
Performance Information   79
   Accumulated Wealth   79
   Quarterly Earnings   80
   Dividend Yield   80
   Price-Earnings Ratio   80
   Return on Investment (ROI)   80
   Return on Equity (ROE)   81
Conclusions   81
Appendix 1   Quick Reference Source   82

5   The Game and the Real World   89

Overview   89
General Conditions   89
Why Differences Exist   89
   The Use of Simple Models   89
   Real-World Models—Difficult to Define   90
   Adopting Theoretically Sound Models   90
Uncertainty in the Game   91
   Producing an Unknown Product   91
   Uncertain Future Product Demand and Price   92
   Operating Leverage and the Game   92
   Financial Leverage and the Game   93
Constraints on Flexibility   94
Decision Requirements   94
Informal Organizational Structure   95
Large and Small Businesses   96
Financial Statement Accounts and Performance   96
   Revenues   96
   Production Costs   99
   Selling and Administrative Expenses   101
   Advertising   101
   Financial Expenses   102
   Taxes   107
   Equities   108
   Performance Information   112
   Extraordinary Items, Fires, and Strikes   117
Conclusion   117

Index   119

FinGame Online 5.0

The Financial Management Decision Game
Participant's Manual

Introduction

Overview

The primary objective of an experiential learning simulation game, such as Fin-Game Online 5.0 (FG), comes from learning how to plan, formulate strategies, and make sets of sound decisions sequentially through time. FG provides a decision-making setting similar in many respects to the financial management requirements of an actual company. The manager of an FG company has the operating control of an entire company. The *manager is the chief financial officer (CFO)* who also controls major decisions normally managed by the *chief executive officer (CEO) and chief operating officer (COO)*.

The FG decision environment is much more complex than the environment found in standard texts and case courses for two primary reasons. First, decisions are entered in many interrelated areas in each period of play. Tools and techniques previously examined, analyzed, and employed in only single-decision problems now must be applied in the presence of interrelationships with many other simultaneously derived decisions.

Second, decisions must be entered over several periods of play. The consequences of prior decisions impact the range of decisions available in later periods. To be successful, an adopted strategy must be flexible enough to adjust to a changing environment over time. Avoiding decisions that eliminate a large set of future company options is key to this flexibility. Additionally and most importantly, FG managers receive direct feedback every period of play on the consequences, good or bad, of their prior decisions. They then commonly need to revise their strategy and plan to adapt to changes in their FG world. This adaptation in strategizing and planning is a primary source of learning in the real world, and generally very costly for the manager and her or his company.

> **Example.** Too much debt and not enough shareholder equity could lead to depressed stock prices. Use of low-priced stock to rebalance the company's debt-equity ratio to a more reasonable level would then be very expensive.

This interrelationship among decisions both at a point in time and over time adds to the complexity of the decision-making setting. To perform successfully, a strategy must be developed that combines the numerous single-decision solution techniques into an effectively integrated set of multiple-period decisions.

The primary objective of FinGame is to learn how to plan, formulate strategies, and make sets of sound decisions sequentially through time.

Material differences exist between the game and an actual environment; these differences are reviewed in Chapter 5. The experience gained in the game is not fully transferable to an actual operating company, but most of the specific problem-solving techniques that lead to successful game performance are transferable. Experience is gained in simultaneously considering a large set of interrelated decisions and integrating this set of decisions into a coherent overall firm strategy. The major purpose of FG is to provide a setting where general decision-making skills in solving complex multiple-period management problems can be experienced and improved.

Business simulation games are usually enthusiastically received. The games require an active role, allowing the practical application of knowledge gained from lectures or other instructional formats. In addition, the success of a firm in the game is directly related to the effort and knowledge of the company managers.

The Financial Management Decision Game (FinGame Online 5.0) is a comprehensive multiple-period finance case requiring up to 20 separate management decisions in each period of play. Most decisions are financial; however, a few nonfinancial decisions are included because they have a major impact on financial decisions.

The Purpose of the Game

Use of the game complements and strengthens student skills in managerial accounting, production, and finance by requiring a repeated application of principles, tools, and procedures learned in each of the disciplines. Sound financial decisions are required concerning the firm's financial structure (liabilities and equity mix) and its resource allocation (asset mix).

To successfully operate a company, an FG company manager must forecast, plan, and control his or her company. Through game play, the manager gets information on the dependence among the different decision variables. The manager must then construct a sound decision-making structure for the firm. The decision tools and techniques that should be used approximate those needed in constructing financial decision-making systems for a real-world operating company.

In summary, much of the participant's learning comes directly from experience gained by operating in the iterative and interactive problem-solving environment provided by the game. The simulation requires decision making in an environment similar to the real world, where new events occur requiring specific new decisions. Also, like a real situation, performance measures reflect the consequences of decisions. The game's characteristics make it an especially pertinent vehicle for demonstrating a complex decision-making setting and providing students with experience in making decisions in this environment.

Text Contents

Students should read the entire manual before making company decisions. The manager who is more knowledgeable about both the firm and its environment will often perform better than a less-informed manager.

Chapter 1 provides an overview of the game. This includes the purpose of the game, an overview of students' primary management objective, a brief description of the game environment, and a suggested procedure for preparing and using the game.

Chapter 2 contains information on how to access and use the web site. Information on initializing the company and the procedures for entering decisions, running the simulation, and viewing or printing results are included.

Chapter 3 discusses the development of a stated, coherent, and integrated strategy or plan for managing a company. The prime directive of the manager is to maximize the wealth of common stockholders. Wealth maximization is achieved, in part, by effectively managing each decision area. Each decision area controlled by the student is reviewed, together with examples of poor and effective management.

There is no single correct policy for maximizing shareholder wealth in the game. The game environment controlled by the instructor determines what the optimal policies of the company should be.

> **Example.**   If the environment is very business cyclical or the company is in a high-growth industry, a smaller amount of debt coupled with larger amounts of shareholder equity leads to better performance relative to a company having proportionally more debt and less equity. The reverse holds for a mature company with little business cyclical risk.

Chapter 4 presents the numerous rules that define the FinGame company's environment. Successful participation in the game by a new company manager requires a complete reading of this manual before the start of game simulations and a thorough understanding of the rules and conditions governing game play.

Chapter 5 compares and contrasts the game and an actual environment since a computer game cannot totally duplicate the conditions of the real world.

An online Appendix available in student accounts contains the procedure for constructing pro forma (budgeted or expected future) company financial statements. The Appendix provides practice in generating the first set of pro forma statements for an FG company. The rules and conditions given in Chapter 4 are used to construct the pro forma statements.

Preparation of the expected future or pro forma statements by hand, and thus a review of the Appendix, is unnecessary if students will be permitted to computer-generate pro forma statements within FinGame. The instructor will specify what participants must do.

Given the case orientation of FinGame, the manual does not contain information on finance models and decision techniques. Students must rely on outside texts and course work for the necessary decision tools.

Planning and forecasting are essential in building a company management strategy.

Students need to read the entire manual before making actual company decisions.

The Game Environment

The environment determines the optimal management policies. Students must rely on outside texts and course work for the necessary decision tools.

Managers act as agents for the common equity holders of the company. Effective managers efficiently acquire and invest funds. In an efficient market, common stockholder value is increased when managers invest in assets that provide a return on investment that exceeds the cost of capital used to make the investment. Common stockholder wealth is decreased when an investment does not earn a sufficient return to cover the cost of funds used to finance the investment. A manager's primary objective in FinGame is to maximize common stockholder wealth.

Note that:

- All FinGame companies produce and sell the same product.
- All companies start the game with the same asset mix, financial structure, and potential for success.

- Each firm is provided with an initial set of financial statements including a position statement (balance sheet), a performance report (income statement), and a statement of additional summary data, which includes additional historical and forecasted information not shown on the standard financial statements. The starting sets of statements and data are identical for all firms.
- A new set of updated financial statements and summary data is generated for each company in each period of play based on the manager's set of company decisions for that period.
- A new set of decisions is required for each period of play.
- The duration of a period of play is equivalent to one-quarter of a year (three months).
- As in the real world, managers cannot repeat an already completed quarter of operation.
- A company has a maximum life of 24 quarters, although most uses of the game cover about 12 quarters of play. The instructor will indicate the number of quarters of play.

A brief description of the operating procedure follows. (Chapter 4 fully explains all operating rules, conditions, and financial statements' contents.) There are many possible decisions. The instructor will state which decisions the manager will control:

1. Units to be produced.
2. Unit price of product.
3. Purchase of demand and price forecast.
4. Plant capacity purchased.
5. Machine capacity purchased.
6. Capital budgeting project A.
7. Capital budgeting project B.
8. Decision on labor strike settlement (if a labor strike is possible next quarter).
9. Short-term investment.
10. Risk of short-term investment.
11. Discount terms on receivables.
12. Advertising expense.
13. Short-term loan.
14. Two-year term loan.
15. Three-year term loan.
16. Long-term debt.
17. Preferred stock.
18. Common stock.
19. Tender price for repurchase.
20. Dividend on common stock.
21. Possible strike settlement.

Game players directly enter decisions on each of the preceding variables that they control. The instructor determines which of the above variables are under players' control and will indicate variables, if any, that managers will not control.

The variables players control also determine other company decisions and conditions on which players do not directly enter decisions.

Example. The production decision will determine the end-of-period inventory balance even though managers do not directly enter an ending inventory decision. Also, all decisions affecting cash flows for the period will determine the ending cash balance. Cash management is determined by the manager even though there is no decision entered for an ending cash balance. Both the inventory and cash balance policies need to be actively controlled by managers. The policies are controlled only by recognizing and managing the active decisions that affect these policies. Cash management is achieved by preparing budgeted or pro forma financial statements, which are described in Chapters 3 and 4.

The game is a multiple-period decision problem. Starting with an identical initial company, each manager makes her/his first set of decisions for quarter 2. The financial statements and summary information on the company received from the simulation of quarter 2 are then used to make decisions for quarter 3. This decision process is replicated for the 11 to 24 quarters of operation for the game. Once the quarter is simulated, decisions for a given quarter cannot be repeated. As in the real world, the company's future is based on prior sets of unchangeable decisions.

The company operates in a nonspecific environment. The company is not a firm in a specific industry, such as chemicals, and it produces an unidentified product. This reduces the manager's possible bias toward using an existing industry's financial structure or asset mix. Game managers should make sound financial decisions based on their company's operating environment rather than rely on decisions and rules of thumb currently used within a specific industry.

Decisions among companies are independent. Neither the decisions nor the performance position of any one firm causes changes in any other firm. No manager's actions will change the overall market equilibrium conditions.

Example. An issuance of stock by company 2 does not change the sales price of company 1 stock. The firms are not competing against each other for a limited amount of product sales, machines, plant, capital budgeting projects, production, or capital.

The environment is very similar to a perfect competition environment, where capital markets are complete and efficient. Each company is too small to have an effect on the market equilibrium interest rate of marketable securities or other firms' costs of capital. General marketwide prices, interest rates, product demand, and costs in the game are all affected by an economic index that is independent of each firm's actions.

Performance is cumulative. The manager's objective is to maximize common stockholders' long-run wealth. This goal is reached by repeatedly making sound financial decisions. Because performance is determined by several decisions in each of several periods, a firm's performance is derived from its entire set of past decisions.

Example. Company A makes the same decisions as company B except A accepts a capital budgeting project that should be rejected and company B rejects the project. Firm B will have operated in the best interests of its shareholders and will outperform A. The difference in decisions between the two firms could result in performance superiority for B that could last the entire game. The full weight of the effect on the financial statements and overall company performance often will not be evident until the end of the life of the capital budgeting project. Company A's costs could exceed B's in each period of the project's life, thus adding cumulatively to B's advantage.

A manager's decisions can have additional indirect and/or secondary effects on operating and financial costs, which in turn further impact the company's performance position.

Example.   Incorrect capital budgeting decisions could lead to a poorly operating firm with a lower stock price and higher debt costs than other firms. This firm could issue new shares and debt only at a higher average cost of funds than obtained by a better firm. The present value or profitability of the same new investments would be lower for the already poorly performing firm. The firm would underperform the more successful companies still further due to this type of secondary valuation effect.

Secondary effects cause further disparities between high- and low-performance companies as the game progresses. This feedback effect can place a company in a "locked-out" position where there is little hope of catching up to better-performing companies. This condition is just like the long-term dominance in performance that exists with some companies in the real world.

The manager operates in an uncertain environment. The manager has incomplete information on the future, lacking knowledge about future company performance, product demand, product price, and interest rates. The capable manager searches for lead indicators (predictors of the future conditions) to decrease the level of uncertainty.

The game is a comprehensive case. The game and this text are constructed like a traditional case. Knowledge in finance, accounting, and other disciplines required for successful company management needs to be obtained from other sources. A finance text can reveal the impact of financial decisions and appropriate solution techniques for solving problems.

Example.   A basic finance course covers the possible impact on a company's cost of capital from either excess debt or excess equity. A manager who lacks this knowledge will likely underperform other company managers. The naïve manager would fail to monitor the effect of the debt-equity relationship on the cost of capital for her/his company and other companies. The manager could fail to adjust debt equity back toward more reasonable levels even in light of clear evidence of a poor policy, thus underperforming the more knowledgeable managers.

The game is interdisciplinary. In a successful company, financial management cannot be separated from decision making in other disciplines of business and economics. The production, marketing, and accounting functions are highly interrelated with the economic environment and optimal financial decisions. A decision or event in one area induces changes in others. Operation of an entire firm requires planning, decision making, and control of all the business management functions in each decision period.

The game is designed with emphasis on finance in that:

1. Most of the decisions are financial variables.
2. Decision requirements on the financial variables are typically more complex than the nonfinancial decisions.
3. The weights of the effects of the finance variables on performance are generally greater than nonfinancial variables.

A limited number of production and marketing decisions are included to increase the game player's awareness of their effects on financial decision making.

A unique set of optimal decisions may not be found or exist. The optimal set of decisions for a company may change over time if the company's environment changes.

Example.   Because of possible shifts in the underlying economy, the environment in which the firm operates is subject to substantial change over time. The capital and asset structure of the firm might have to be modified to ensure a company's continued

Decisions of any single company do not affect any other company. Decisions often have major secondary effects for the company.

high performance. A strategy incorporating high financial leverage might be appropriate for a highly stable firm. Yet, if the firm moves toward greater business instability, maintaing high financial leverage could cause failure or at least relatively poorer performance.

Effective financial decisions must be integrated with nonfinancial management decisions.

Since performance in the game is cumulative, to fully understand the impact of a single variable, the manager must explain its relationship among the many other company variables, the feedback effects among the variables, and how this feedback is affected by time. Additionally, due to the uncertainty in the game environment, much of the information required to determine the impact of one decision variable and the relationships among the variables is not observable or measurable.

As in the real world, decisions must still be made in this uncertain environment with the objective of maximizing common stockholders' wealth. The manager should seek information and make decisions through several periods of play in an attempt to approach an optimal decision for each manager-controlled variable.

> **Example.**   Dividends affect stock price and the performance measure in the game. The company's manager knows this but does not know the relationship between payout and performance. By varying dividend payout throughout the game and examining the impact of other companies' dividend policies, management can hone in on the optimal or near-optimal payout.

Effective financial management requires repeated analysis of the impact from a given decision variable. In this environment, a decision is tested and the effect on performance is measured. This process continues until an optimal solution or optimal range of solutions is determined and implemented for a given management decision variable, such as dividend policy.

If the general economic environment did not change through time and if the firm could be simulated through hundreds or thousands of periods, the optimal set or sets of management decision variables could be estimated fairly accurately. Due to the rapid changes in the real world and the game, firms rarely have the number of stable periods necessary to discover the entire set of optimal decisions. A restricted number of 11 to 24 periods in a game more closely duplicates the real-world experience of managing a company with an insufficient number of periods to derive an optimal solution on all decision variables.

Preparation Requirements

Knowledge of finance, accounting, economics, and production is required of a FinGame manager. The manager has to master the areas sufficiently to apply them in making decisions. More specifically, the operation of a company requires:

1. Understanding of current theory in both finance and economics.
2. Knowledge of financial statements, their construction, and the specific impacts on the statements resulting from each possible management decision.
3. Ability to apply established analytical methods to problem solving in finance; for example, in capital budgeting the manager should know how to apply the net present value or internal rate of return procedures.
4. Ability to communicate financial information.

An understanding of basic finance and economics is essential. Economic training will enable the manager to guess how interest rates, product demand, and prices of both input material and the final product should correlate with the general business cycle.

Knowledge of finance provides models that explain the impacts on the firm's earnings stream from increasing either financial or operating leverage, the effects of dividend stability and payout on stock prices, and the means of determining an optimal sales discount for credit sales. Stock-out and economic order quantity models can be used in decisions about cash levels, inventory levels, and purchasing machine and plant capacity. The net present value or internal rate of return method can be applied to capital budgeting and debt refunding decisions. This type of information will guide the new company manager in forming an initial set of decisions.

The substantial flow of information from each iteration of the game will either reinforce or deny the soundness of the models initially adopted and should, when necessary, lead the manager to refine, modify, or replace the models used when making future decisions.

An understanding of both the content and the construction of financial statements is a prerequisite to financial analysis and management. A physician would be ineffective without a comprehensive knowledge of anatomy. Likewise, a financial manager without a comprehensive understanding of financial statements and an ability to analyze them would be ineffective. Only with this knowledge could the manager make a good diagnosis of a company's problems and select appropriate corrective actions. A thorough knowledge of financial statements enhances managers' ability to both construct statements and judge the impact of financial decisions on their statements.

Prior beliefs are validated or denied by new evidence.

Web Access and Use

Overview

The FinGame Online web site is listed on the user registration code card supplied inside the front cover of the FinGame Online manual. The web site contains the simulation for a hypothetical company that will be active on the www.mhhe.com web site for six months from the initial login of the account. The simulation covers up to 24 periods of operation. The FinGame (FG) manager makes numerous irrevocable financial and production decisions each period. Each period is equal to managing the company for a three-month interval, or a quarter. The manager receives information on the performance and position of the company after each simulation of the most recently entered quarterly set of decisions. Managers use this information along with future forecast information to formulate company decisions for future quarters. Information on all previously simulated quarters is retained for viewing and printing from the web site.

Most instructors also allow students to use the FG simulation to prepare estimated or budgeted statements, which are called pro forma statements in FinGame and many real companies. Pro forma statements enable students to estimate the consequences of their decisions before using these decisions for the actual nonreversible quarter simulation. Chapter 3 provides the process for preparing appropriate pro forma statements and then using the information from the final adopted pro forma for the actual quarter's decisions.

Computer Requirements

System requirements include a Web browser, including Microsoft Internet Explorer 6 and 7 and Firefox 1.5 or above. Broadband Internet is recommended. Initial loading will take a couple of minutes on dial-up connections, but thereafter will be almost instant if stored in the browser's cache. Then significant wait times are unlikely once logged in. A printer is also required if hard copy quarterly game output is desired.

Initial Instructions

Participants do not make actual decisions for quarter 1.

Quarter 1 in FG generates the starting company, which is the same for all game participants. Participants will not make any management decisions for quarter 1. The game participant will need to run the simulation for quarter 1 if the instructor has not already simulated the first quarter; she or he will indicate if students will need to run quarter 1. This process is required to *"Initialize"* the starting company and generate the starting set of financial statements. *The student/manager's first active set of decisions for the company will be for quarter 2.*

The instructor will provide the following specific critical information needed to operate FG.

- The instructor will provide the appropriate **Join a Group** entry code that is required to sign into the group of companies.
- Three options exist on enabling students to simulate each new quarter in FG. The instructor will indicate which option will be used.
  1. The instructor provides a unique three-digit alphanumeric quarterly "advance code" that allows participants to run a specific nonrepeatable quarterly simulation of the game. For example the code for quarter 5 might be "N?7." This code must be entered before the simulation of actual quarter 5 decisions can be performed.
  2. The instructor initiates the running of the simulation for a given quarter, providing instructions on when this will be done for each quarter. All decisions need to be entered and saved for the quarter before the instructor runs the simulation.
  3. Students can advance at any time they choose to the next quarter without permission in the form of either an advance code or instructor-initiated simulation.

- The instructor will provide the rules for naming the company if the FG company's management will have more than one student. When one student will manage each company, the student's name will generally be required to name the company. Follow the instructor's instructions.
- The instructor may select a different environment for the company than the environment included on the web site or in this manual. In either case, quarter 1 financial statements and summary data will differ from the ones presented in Exhibits 4.1, 4.2, 4.3 in Chapter 4. Use the actual quarter 1 statements generated in FG to determine the company's initial position, performance, and future characteristics. Use of the forecasts and conditions in the Chapter 4 exhibits would be faulty and could cause serious performance losses.

The following instructions for initiating an FG account can be performed before obtaining any of the above information. Familiarity with the menus, practice in making decision entries, experience in running financial planning simulations (if permitted by the instructor) and examining results can be practiced. Participants will not be able to run an actual quarterly simulation unless the above option 3 is adopted by the instructor.

Getting a Company Account

To register and create a new FinGame company account, go to http://www.mhhe .com/fingame5 and select the "Click Here to Activate a New Account" option (Screen 1). Follow the directions on entering the registration key code at the front of this manual and other required account information including your own FinGame user name and password. Thereafter, your new user name and password will be entered on Screen 1 to access your account. You will not be able to access all of FinGame's options until you enter your group code that will be provided by your instructor.

Operating a FinGame Company

All major options and activities are initiated from the main menu screen.

Once the company account is established, full access to the company's environment and decisions will be available, subject to any restrictions placed on the operation of the company by the instructor. Access to the initial actual quarter 1 statements and quarter 2 decisions may not be available, and actual quarter play may not be possible, until the instructor initiates all companies' starting position at quarter 1. If the **Current company quarter** is at 0 [zero] this condition holds.

1. Go to http://mhhe.com/fingame5 and select "Login to FinGame."
2. Enter your user name and password.
3. The main menu screen of the FinGame company's account will appear. **Warning!** Using the web browser's back page button will exit the account and a new user name would be needed. Prior unsaved information would be lost. This occurs because a FinGame account has only the single main menu page and all selected options add new material and remove prior material from this same page.

SCREEN 1   New Account Registration and Existing Account Login

FinGame 5.0

Login to an existing account:

User name: [   ]

Password: [   ]

[Sign in to an Existing Account]

Help with problems logging in
[Click Here to Activate a New Account]

Beta version 1.65

4. If the student has not yet joined the instructor's group, a "Join a Group" option will be present. If you have not yet done so, select the "Join a Group" option to enter the instructor-provided code to access most of the main menu options.

5. "Account Settings" allows changes in the user name, password, establishment or modification of a company name, and personal information.

6. "Edit Pro Forma Decision Inputs" allows preparation of budgeted or estimated statements that are generated from the company's current financial position based on the manager's forecasts of estimated units of product demanded, estimated interest rates for the coming period, and the remaining set of company operating, investment, and financing decisions. When completed, execute "Save Changes" for them to be retained. Details on preparing sound pro forma statements are in Chapter 3.

7. The "Run Pro Forma Simulation" option is used to generate the pro forma financial statements and summary data based on the preceding step.

8. "View Pro Forma Results" enables the viewing of the simulated information for the current and all prior completed company quarters generated in step 7. The results contain information similar to Exhibits 4.1, 4.2, and 4.3 in Chapter 4. Only the most recently simulated set of pro forma statements generated will be retained. A prior set of pro forma statements will be overwritten whenever a new pro forma simulation is run. The last pro forma run before the actual quarter run is retained in each company's history file and can be viewed on all prior quarters and the current quarter.

9. Students can replicate steps 6 to 8 as often as they like. With an appropriate planning algorithm, the final plan should be achieved within two to four iterations of steps 6 to 8. Only the most recent set of pro forma statements are retained on the web site. Saving the html file or a print copy of each pro forma is advised during early game play in order to trace planning errors.

10. With the final plan from item 9, go to "Edit Actual Decision Inputs."

11. The decisions from the final pro forma plan in step 9 are automatically transferred to the actual decision inputs shown upon entering the "Edit Actual Decision Inputs" screen.

12. Next, "Run [the] Actual Simulation" to generate the financial statements and summary data for the actual quarter.

13. "View Actual Results" enables viewing of the quarter's simulation results generated by step 12. The results contain information like that presented in Exhibits 4.1, 4.2, and 4.3 in Chapter 4. Any prior actual quarterly set of statements can be viewed by selecting the desired quarter number from this option.

14. When the session is completed, select the "Logout" option to end the online session. No information about the company will be on the student's computer unless the student saves copies of the html screens that are being viewed.

15. Steps 1 through 14, excluding step 3, are repeated for each period of play assigned by the instructor.

Details on Main Menu Options

Basic Account Information

The top line of the main menu (Screen 2), from left to right, contains the student supplied university or organization name, the instructor's group name, the most recently completed actual quarter simulation, and the student's user name. The "Account Settings" option provides the company account information and enables implementation of other unique FG features described here. The set of items includes the **User name, E-mail** address, **Company name**, and the ability to reset other initial required registration information.

Change User Name

Students can change the initial default user name provided in the manual to a name of their choice. This must be a unique name on the web site; an alert will indicate if an alternative is needed. The user name also can be changed later. The company name need not be unique among all FinGame users on the system.

Change Password

The password can also be changed. Access to the web site is not possible without a user name and password. If students forget these two key items of information, the instructor can look up the user name and then issue a new password.

Enabling Other Unique FG Features

Most of the options for changing account information are self-explanatory. The ones that are likely unique to FG are now defined.

View Other Companies.   The instructor can enable participants to view the financial statements of other group members. The company number and name and its accumulated wealth are provided through the current quarter for all companies. The instructor will determine the number of quarters that must elapse before a company's statements will be publicly available to the other group members. The most common delay selected by instructors is one quarter so that a company has private information for one quarter of a FinGame year before the statements become public information. This is reasonably equivalent to real-world companies. In the United States, the Securities and Exchange Commission (SEC) requires 10Q

SCREEN 2   **FinGame Main Menu**

(quarterly) statements to be filed and publicly available two and one-half months after the quarter is completed. Thus, FG's one-quarter delay before access is available is only two weeks longer than the real-world standard.

Add a View Group.   If the instructor provides a **View group code** to look at the results of other companies, the "Add a view group" option is used to enter the **View group code** allowing access to the above "" option.

Supplemental Materials.   Supplemental files described elsewhere in the participant's manual and additional new documents will be posted here that may be downloaded. Your instructor will indicate any required or recommended files that need to be covered.

Process for Quarterly Company Simulations

Edit Pro Forma Decision Inputs

Pro forma (projected or budgeted) statements test the impact of decisions.

Screen 3 shows the first panel of the **Pro Forma Decision Sheet** that appears only when the "Edit Pro Forma Decision Inputs" option is selected from the main menu. This section of the decision entry form requires that the company manager forecast expected demand, interest rates for securities for the coming quarter, and the product unit price. Screens 4 through 6 contain the remaining components of the decision entry form. Decisions on Screens 4 through 6 are required for both pro forma decisions and actual quarter decisions.

Pro forma decisions enable a budgeted or projected set of statements of what the company position and performance might look like with a specific set of decisions and environmental conditions. Pro forma statements are required for sound management of the company. Pro forma statements enable the manager to plan better by providing advance estimates of what the company's financial statements would look like for a quarter. Specific instructions on the rules governing the financial and production decisions are contained in Chapter 4, "The Company Environment and Rules."

When all entries have been made satisfactorily for either a pro forma or actual quarterly decision set, the "Save Changes" key is pressed to save the decisions at the web site. Note: The simulation is *not* performed when the decisions are submitted. The decisions entered are stored at the site. The "Edit Pro Forma Decision Inputs" option can still be selected to reenter a new set of decisions that will replace those already submitted. The decision sets can be changed, simulated, and viewed and/or printed and resubmitted until either the manager or the instructor runs the actual quarter's simulation.

When a set of pro forma decisions is ready for simulation, the "Run Pro Forma Simulation" option is selected. The "View Pro Forma Results" option is used to view the simulation results on the most recent pro forma set of decisions simulated at any time until the next pro forma for the same period is simulated. Printed copies or html files should be saved early in the game on every set of pro forma statements simulated to enable a tracing of planning or entry errors.

Pro forma statements can be repeated as often as desired for a given quarter.

A manager can simulate as many sets of pro forma decisions as desired before entering the final set of decisions used to irrevocably advance the company a quarter in time. Pro forma statements in the FG environment can be generated only for the next quarter.

SCREEN 3   Pro Forma Decision Sheet

Pro Forma Decision Sheet for Quarter 2	
Units demanded	
Short term investments	0.00%
Short term loan	0.00%
Three-year loan	0.00%
Preferred stock yield	0.00%
Capital gains rate	0.00%
Two year loan	0.00%
Long-term loan	0.00%

SCREEN 4   Company Operating Decisions for Quarter 1

Company Operating Decisions	
Number of units to produce	
Per unit price	$0.00
Dividends per share of common stock	$0.00
Advertising costs per period	$0
Demand/price forecast	Free
Sales discount	None

SCREEN 5   New Investment Decisions

New Investment Decisions	
Short-term investment	
Risk of short-term investment	0
Units of machinery purchased	
Units of plant purchased	
Capital budgeting project A	no
Capital budgeting project B	no

SCREEN 6   Financing Decisions

Financing Decisions	
DEBT:	
Short-term loans	$0
Two-year loans	$0
Three-year loans	$0
Ten-year bonds	$0
EQUITY:	
Preferred shares	
Common shares	
Common tender price	$0.00
Save Changes	

Example.   The impact of variations in product demand on company income could be examined. This is achieved by examining the same set of company decisions while varying demand levels with different sets of pro forma decisions. The printed pro forma decision results from the set of runs could then be viewed to estimate the impact of demand variations on company income. Alternatively, or in addition, three new sets of pro forma decisions could be used to determine the impact of three different financing sources on net income and cash balances.

Edit Actual Decision Inputs

Unless simulated by the instructor, actual and pro forma decisions ***must be simulated*** with the two "Run Simulation" options.

Actual quarter decisions shown on Screens 4, 5, and 6 are entered and saved with the "Save Changes" key. If pro forma decisions have been entered and saved for the quarter, they will automatically be shown in the decision input boxes when entering the **Edit Actual Decision Inputs** screens. If pro forma statements are not being used, actual decisions will have to be entered as inputs, shown by the variables in Screens 4 through 6. If managers do not have control of a decision, the actual decision input field will not be available, and a text statement will indicate the condition that applies. Specific instructions on the rules governing the financial and production decisions are contained in Chapter 4.

Run Actual Simulation

Actual quarter decisions are irrevocable after the simulation is run.

The simulation of actual decisions is irrevocable. For example, if the manager wrongly failed to enter any units to produce, it is too late. The quarter is now over and the company produced zero units over the past three months. The actual performance and company position now, regrettably, represent the company's current standing. The company does not advance when the decisions are submitted (saved at the web site). The simulation must be "run" with the "Run Actual Simulation" option, or run by the instructor before the decisions made in the "Edit Actual Decision Inputs" option are irrevocable for the specific quarter. The "View Actual Results" option allows a viewing of the actual quarterly statements on all completed quarters at any time.

The Underlying Simulation

The simulation is the program and set of underlying finance and environment models at the heart of FG, where the previously entered decisions (actual or pro forma) are simulated in the FG environment. In this step the following information is processed and events occur.

- The historical financial, production, and performance information and the current position of the company (represented by the current quarterly financial statements) provide the simulation with the information that represents the specific company.
- Information both known and unknown to the manager about the forthcoming quarter's product demand, product price, market interest rates, inflation, plant and machine costs, and other economy-wide economic factors define the simulation environment external to the company.
- The simulation combines the above company and environment information and integrates this information with the manager's specific decisions for the

quarter to determine how the company's position is modified and how the company performs.

- The information in the prior step is used to derive the next quarterly set of financial statements and determine the company's performance.
- The set of actual or pro forma statements formed in the last step is recorded and saved. Updated specific company information, such as future levels of plant capacity for the next 20 quarters, is also recorded and saved.

3 Establishing a Management Plan

Overview

A company's successful management is achieved through its overall strategy and resulting current and future detailed planning. In addition, changes within the company and in its external environment require capable managers to continuously review the company's strategy and modify it to accommodate change. Planning must also reflect these shifts in strategy. This chapter describes how a strategy is formed, managed, and modified over time. The chapter also details the formation of a strategy for managing all the separate decision areas that managers control in FG and it covers the integration of the set of separate decisions into a coherent and well-structured total company strategy.

Accumulated Wealth

The primary objective of the manager as the agent for the common stockholders is to maximize their wealth. In FG *accumulated wealth* per common share of stock (upper right corner of each quarterly summary data sheet) represents common stockholder wealth maximization. The quality of the manager's stewardship of the company is best measured by the value of accumulated wealth. **Accumulated wealth** in FG equals:

- The current value of one share of stock.
- Plus the value of all per share cash dividends distributed from quarter 1 in the game.
- Plus a market rate of interest on all previous dividends and interest on the prior dividends.

The interest represents opportunity gains received externally in lieu of returns that would have been received if the funds had been invested within the company. If the risk-adjusted return earned on the prior paid dividends is greater than the internal firm's return, the prior dividends were justified. These three items represent the *wealth* that a common stockholder would *accumulate* from owning a single original share purchased at the beginning of the game.

How Is Accumulated Wealth Maximized?

One manager outperforms another by:

The primary managerial objective is to maximize common stockholder accumulated wealth.

- Having a superior long-term plan for the management of the company.
- Being flexible in revising the plan quickly and appropriately in response to a changing environment.
- "Micromanaging" each of the company's assets, liabilities, revenues, and costs to minimize long-term costs while maximizing long-term revenues.
- Making new investments if there is an expected value gain (positive net present value) for the company.

For management to be successful, these four performance factors need to be simultaneously managed for each quarter in the game. Relatively stronger management in each area gives the manager a competitive advantage over competing companies that have less capable managers.

This chapter guides FG managers in forming their strategy, which requires a company plan that maintains flexibility. This chapter does not describe the strategy that should be adopted—that task is the FG manager's sole responsibility and primary task.

The rationale for developing a strategy that is embodied in the company plan and the dangers of failing to form a company plan are presented first. The formation of a plan of attack in managing an FG company appears in the following section. The effects of a company's life cycle position and risk-bearing position are considered at the end of the chapter.

The Need for a Company Strategy

In the game as well as in the real world, a capable manager effectively controls his or her company. Control is maintained and implemented with a management plan that represents the strategy. Management's possible set of future reactions to the possible environments must be part of the current plan. **Strategy** is the art of devising or employing plans to achieve a goal. Another dictionary definition is that a strategy is a complex set of adaptations that enable evolutionary success. The essence of a sound strategy is that it is adaptive, or flexible, adjusting to changes in the environment. In FG both the survival of a company and its competitive advantage would be the measure of evolutionary success. The accumulated wealth measure best gauges this success.

The manager establishes an intermediate or long-term strategy and operating plan for running the company based on a realistic perception of the company's current position, its future options, and the potential consequences of adopting given options. The effective plan is flexible, including alternative appropriate future company actions that can be matched to the possible changes in the environment. A sound strategy also permits the manager to modify the plan to accommodate uncontrollable and unexpected changes in the environment.

An undesirable alternative management style follows a reactive role: The manager reacts to changes in the environment after they occur. The more effective the plan, the more the manager controls the company to accommodate a changing environment.

A manager's mastery of an ever-changing environment is not possible due to its uncertainty. The uncertainty comes from imperfect estimation, the impact from other conditions not controllable by the manager, and externally imposed constraints that restrict the manager's actions.

> **Example.**   Managers in FG have no control over the general level of product demand, interest rates, capital budgeting projects offered, basic labor costs, material costs, inventory carrying costs, and numerous other items. Most of these factors also cannot be predicted perfectly. Likewise, constraints exist so that managers cannot sell excess plant and machinery, retire short-term loans before maturity, or issue cash dividends on common stock when preferred stock cash dividends are in arrears.

The uncontrollable variables and externally imposed constraints lead the responsible manager to develop a strategy that has the flexibility to accommodate uncontrollable events without seriously jeopardizing either firm performance relative to other competitors or, in an extreme case, survival of the firm.

Students starting FG are often confused by the seemingly endless set of rules and conditions. Anxiety runs high because the new manager is expected to meld the complex set of rules into a logical, coherent company plan. The same problem occurs in the real world when a new manager enters an actual environment that is far more complex than the game. The next section provides characteristics of a sound plan.

A Plan of Attack in FinGame Online

The discussion that follows uses a building block approach to define a company strategy and implement a company plan. This section describes what needs to be accomplished and provides rudimentary information on the management of each of the decision areas controlled by the manager.

Much of the detailed information on how to make each decision is not provided. Finance texts, lectures by instructors, and management planning teams may provide the specific details. The objective is clear—the manager must develop a plan that maximizes shareholder wealth.

First, each of the major decision areas that the manager controls is examined. Next, the manager must determine an overall company strategy. This strategy will integrate the separate decisions into a unified set. The set of decisions serves as the company management plan. Decisions in a given area cannot be finalized until the integration stage is completed. This condition holds because the optimal decisions in one area affect other decisions.

> **Example.**   The decision on setting the price of the units sold is a multiple-stage problem that affects the optimal level of other decisions. First, when managers control their product's unit sales price, they must determine the effect of setting higher versus lower unit sales prices than the market price. If demand is price-inelastic, price increases lead to relatively smaller decreases in units demanded. Profits and accumulated wealth increase when the higher optimal unit pricing is found and used. Optimal production capacity levels will be lower. With further testing and analysis, managers try to determine the optimal combination of unit price, machine and plant capacity levels, and optimal inventory levels. The possible savings generated from capital budgeting projects are reduced since there is a lower optimal production level. Previously profitable projects might now be unacceptable.
>
> Alternatively, if demand is price-elastic, optimal pricing is lower. Testing and analysis are needed to find the optimal decrease in price. Simultaneously, the required optimal levels of machine and plant capacity increase, optimal inventory level increases, and marginal capital budgeting projects are likely to be more profitable.

The interrelationships among decisions have to be considered in any plan.

A Possible Planning Approach

The following procedure provides one possible approach to developing the company strategy or plan:

- Managers must first seek information on the effects of each possible decision that they control by testing the decision's impact on company position and performance.
- The other management-controllable decisions that would be affected by a given decision, and the nature of the effects, need to be investigated by the manager.
- Once the interrelationship among decisions is estimated or known, managers must forecast the effects of different possible combinations of the interrelated decisions on the future position and performance of the company. Pro forma (budgeted) financial statements are a common tool used in this analysis. Analytical models and solution procedures from finance texts are also often required.
- The best plan developed in the prior step is next implemented in an actual set of quarterly decisions.
- Results from implementing the plan are analyzed.
- If results differ markedly from what was expected, the manager may need to return to the first step and formulate a new plan.
- If results follow expectations, the manager needs to continue to monitor the environment and performance in the future for changes that may require revisions in the plan. For example, a change in the income tax rate affects numerous changes from projects' net present value to the company's weighted average cost of funds.

Using the above process, the manager develops a plan for the company. Current and future estimated possible sets of management decisions will implement this plan. Managers need to plan for each of the major classes of decisions in FG that are considered next. Interrelationships with other codependent decisions must be simultaneously examined. A more extensive plan of attack is examined in this chapter's subsection "Integrating the Set of Decisions." Chapter 4 details the full set of rules on the decisions that follow.

The Need for Pro Forma Statements

The prior approach to developing a plan critically relies on the use of budgeted, or pro forma, financial statements. Planning requirements rightfully occupy a large amount of an effective manager's time. The most recent actual financial statements provide information on the firm's current liquidity, performance, and company position. The statements are a starting point for the financial planning and control processes of a well-managed company. A set of pro forma (or budgeted) financial statements is then constructed from historical statements and management plans, which are founded on the company's current strategic plan.

Using only historical financial statements as a basis for company decisions would be analogous to trying to drive a car when you can only see through the rearview mirror. You can see where you have been, but you cannot tell where you are going.

Pro forma statements are based on future known and estimated information and provide a simulation of where your firm will be under a given set of decisions and environmental conditions. Since the set of decisions is defined by the

Sound planning is iterative. New information is always sought to improve the plan.

manager's strategy (or plan), the pro forma statements enable managers to estimate their company's future position, performance, and liquidity. Comparisons of pro forma statements over different strategies will lead to the rejection of many strategies and narrow a manager's decision to the few strategies that are most likely to maximize common shareholders' wealth.

A set of projected, or pro forma, statements shows the estimated effects of both management-controlled and -uncontrolled variables on the future performance and position of the firm. The pro forma statements often disclose previously unforeseen problems that require the manager to revise a prior set of tentative decisions. Otherwise, irreversible and undesirable expensive commitments can be made.

For control purposes, after the quarter is over, the manager should compare previous pro forma statements with actual statements. Discrepancies should be measured and evaluated. A change in both forecasting and decision techniques might be indicated. This will improve future pro forma statement accuracy and result in better planning of future company performance.

At the instructor's discretion, participants will be permitted to generate pro forma statements on the web site. If the manager has this capability, more management plans can be tried since it takes much less time than hand-generating additional sets of pro forma statements. Examining multiple possible plans, or sets of decisions, is called *flexible budgeting*. Flexible budgeting is nearly universally used in the business world.

Cash and Liquidity Management

Sound cash and liquidity management requires minimizing the combination of carrying costs and stock-out costs for cash. In FG the cost of capital invested in cash balances determines the carrying cost for cash.

The stock-out costs for cash have two tiers. At the end of a quarter, the cash balance is determined. If the cash balance is negative, cash is brought in to provide a positive ending cash balance. Any marketable securities outstanding are liquidated at a 3 percent discount rate to cover the cash shortage. A penalty loan with an 8 percent quarterly interest rate is issued to overcome any remaining cash shortfall. Stock-out costs then equal the marketable securities discount less any interest earned for the quarter on the securities liquidated plus the interest cost on penalty loans.

Optimal management minimizes the combination of carrying and stock-out costs. Use pro forma statements to maintain effective cash management.

With optimal cash balance maintenance, the long-run average carrying costs would equal the long-run average stock-out costs. For most economic environments of an FG company, the average cash balance can be maintained at less than $150,000 when there are no marketable securities outstanding. Pro forma financial statements should be used to see if sufficient, but not excessive, funds are being secured in a quarter to take care of the quarterly investments and cash flow needs of the company.

The earnings rate on marketable securities is well below the average FG company's cost of capital, making them a poor (equivalent to a negative net present value) investment. Permanent balances in the marketable securities account would be inconsistent with accumulated wealth maximization. Marketable securities might be appropriate for temporary storage of excess funds that will be needed in the short-term future.

Example.   The company may issue bonds to pay for current plant capacity additions and machinery capacity additions that will take place next quarter. Because there is a fixed fee of $50,000 to issue bonds, for economic order quantity (EOQ) reasons, a single issue may be preferred to an issue in both quarters. A larger current issue would avoid the $50,000 fee next period. The excess funds needed in the next period could be invested in marketable securities and earn interest not gained if the funds were kept as cash balances.

This example demonstrates the interrelationship among decisions. Since the marketable securities earn less than the cost of capital, the shortfall between the two represents a loss of wealth to common stockholders that must be more than offset by the EOQ advantage of eliminating an extra $50,000 order cost. If not, two bond offerings would be desired and the temporary investment in marketable securities avoided.

Other Interrelationships.   Cash and cash balances are determined by the entire set of other decision variables controlled by the manager. This is why the use of pro forma financial statements is critical in the management of cash and liquidity. See "Integrating the Set of Decisions" subsection later in this chapter for details on maintaining adequate liquidity.

Capital Budgeting Analysis

Managers need to evaluate two new A and B projects available in *each* quarter with standard capital budgeting analysis procedures. A text should be used to review the procedures and theory underlying capital budgeting decisions. The projects are independent of each other, and standard net present value analysis (NPV) is appropriate.

Managers need to estimate the labor savings over the 8-quarter life of an A project and the 12-quarter life of a B project. Labor savings come from up to the first 100,000 units of product produced with an A project and up to 120,000 units with a B project. Forecasts of unit demand for the next four quarters are available from the quarterly financial information generated by FG.

Managers must estimate the demand for the remaining four quarters for an A project and eight quarters for a B project. As in the real world for many companies, accurate forecasts for more than a year in the future are often unavailable. At the start of the game, the manager might use the average unit demand for the first four quarters as the estimate for still future quarters. A more refined estimate can possibly be made if more information indicates a consistent pattern of unit demand over time.

NPV derivation requires per period cash flows for project A or B. The following are used to get period cash flows:

Capital budgeting projects need evaluation with NPV analysis. Project savings have to be estimated for each quarter.

- At project inception, the only cash flow is the project cost. This will be called point zero in time for capital budgeting analysis and represents the point at the start of the next quarter of company operation.
- In each operating period (1 through 8 for A or 1 through 12 for B) the labor savings must be determined. The estimated number of units to be produced (no greater than A's or B's capacity level) is multiplied by the labor savings per unit for the specific quarter to get the quarter's labor savings. The labor savings is a cost reduction and cash inflow.
- The overhead savings for A is a positive cash flow. Overhead costs increase for B are a quarterly cash outflow.
- Depreciation is a tax-deductible expense and is straight-line in FG. The per-period depreciation is calculated by dividing the initial project cost by 8 for an A project or by 12 for a B project.
- The sum of the labor savings (+), overhead change (+ for A or − for B), and depreciation (−) equals the pretax quarterly income generated by the project.

- The tax rate times the pretax income equals the quarterly tax cash flow.
- Income before taxes less the tax equals the per-period net income after tax contribution of the project.
- The net cash flow for each of the 8 or 12 operating quarters is equal to the net income after taxes plus the depreciation that had previously been subtracted when calculating taxable income.

The preceding information provides a net period cash flow for 0 through 8 for A projects or 0 through 12 for B projects. Cash flows for quarters 1 through 12 must next be discounted at the quarterly marginal cost of capital rate to be described in the next subsection. The initial cost and present value of future quarter flows are added to derive the project's NPV. If the NPV is greater than zero, the project returns more than an adequate rate of return and the project should be accepted. If the NPV is negative, the project should be rejected.

Capital Structure and Weighted Average Cost of Capital

A text is needed to mathematically derive the weighted average cost of capital (WACC) and to review theory on optimal capital structure. The WACC represents the opportunity or discount rate used to evaluate the company's average risk investments. In the real world as in FG, managers want to minimize capital costs and maximize common stockholder wealth. These goals are supported with an optimal capital structure of debt to equity capital.

The FG company is in a new industry and an "acceptable" industrywide optimal debt-equity ratio is not known. Possible prerequisites for the existence of an optimal capital structure include taxes, bankruptcy costs, agency costs, and asymmetric information between managers and investors. Without some of these conditions, financial leverage may not affect company value. The required conditions for an optimal capital structure exist in FG.

Setting and managing the debt-equity ratio to minimize the cost of capital in FG is a continuous process. Costs of funds of the manager's company and competitors' companies need to be monitored. The manager needs to be ready to modify the target capital structure if evidence mounts that the company's costs of capital are excessive. This monitoring in FG comes from examining the rates on funding in the next quarter that are on the company's quarterly summary data statement. A revision in the target debt-equity ratio is likely called for if the company's WACC is increasing or increasing relative to other FG companies.

The objective is to minimize the cost of capital.

An optimal target debt equity ratio changes if the business risk of the company changes.

The optimal WACC in FG is a function of the volatility of the company's earnings and earnings growth rate. Manager decisions affect both factors. The optimal capital structure can vary among companies operating in the same FG environment. The instructor also modifies the economy faced by all companies each term—the optimal capital structure that may have been appropriate in the past might not apply for the current FG environment, which may have different levels of business cyclical risk, volatility, and long-term growth rates.

Managers will need to estimate the company's WACC to be used as the discount or hurdle rate for company investments (asset purchases). For example, the WACC would be the correct discount rate used in an NPV analysis of projects A and B each quarter. Plant and machinery purchases also must be expected to cover the WACC. The WACC rate also can be used as the carrying cost of invested funds to be used in cash and inventory level decisions and debt refunding decisions. However, since these decisions are less risky than the fixed asset decisions, an alternative risk-adjusted discount (RAD) rate that is lower than the WACC may be more appropriate. See a basic finance text for more detail on the importance and use of an RAD method.

The combination of financing of short-term, two-year, and three-year debt as well as bonds determines the maturity mix of debt. The manager controls the mix based on risk and cost differences of the various debt instruments. With a typical positively sloped yield curve, the cost of debt increases with maturity. Managers can reduce average debt cost by decreasing the maturity of their company debt. The trade-off for the lower debt cost is the higher risk resulting from a decrease in possible future liquidity.

> **Example.**   Average debt costs are reduced with a positively sloped yield curve by using more short-term and two-year debt and less bonds and three-year debt. Managers then have the added responsibility of having to return to the debt markets much more often to refinance the greater quantity of maturing debt. This requires both more planning and the risk of having to refinance in all possible conditions. If the economy and company perform poorly, managers must still externally acquire funds at any cost to replace the shortfall in available funds caused by the larger payments on maturing debt.

In FG there is also a possible gain and risk with bond financing. On the plus side, the manager can lock in an interest rate for the 10-year or 40-quarter life of the bonds. If expectations are that interest rates will be higher for the company in the future, and the market debt costs have not yet captured this expected increase, managers can get windfall gains for their common stockholders by issuing the low-cost bonds. For example, this condition would hold when managers have information on deterioration of the company's future performance not yet known by investors. Real-world evidence confirms the existence of this behavior, which can also profitably be used in FG.

On the negative side, issuing a bond also locks the manager into a long-term source of financing. If interest rates go down, debt holders gain wealth and common stockholders lose wealth since they are now paying too high an interest rate for debt. Refunding bonds in FG, as in the real world, is costly. An 8 percent call premium is required in FG to call bonds before maturity. Call premiums do not exist for the other possible debt instruments.

The most difficult item to estimate in calculating the cost of capital is the cost of common stock. The FG company has no recorded history available when the manager gets control of the company. Yet, most cost of common stock models require historical or future expected information for many periods when deriving percent cost estimates. As in the real world, decisions still have to be made and a cost of common stock must be estimated.

The FG company, like a real-world company in a new industry, lacks the precedence of an already existing company with similar products that could be used to estimate the cost of capital and common stock. This "pure play" approach would often enable a new company to derive cost of common stock and cost of capital estimates.

The manager does know that securities in a company have different risk levels. Debt is safer than preferred stock, and preferred stock is safer than common stock. FG does provide estimates of the future costs of debt and preferred stock, but no estimate of common stock. The manager can use this known relationship among security costs to derive a proxy estimate of the cost of common stock. Until the manager gets better information, a simple rule of thumb would be to use the cost of preferred stock plus a premium equal to the difference between bond cost and preferred stock cost as an estimate of the cost of common stock.

Other Interrelationships. The company cost of capital reflects the environment and all prior management decisions.

Example. Poor liquidity management could lead to excessive total costs of maintaining cash balances, thereby reducing company profitability relative to other companies. Errors in faulty NPV analysis with prior A and B projects resulting in accepted decisions with negative NPVs and rejected decisions with positive NPVs also decrease profitability and company wealth. Both types of conditions would leave the company less profitable, and with proportionally greater underperformance in bad times, it would be more risky than its more capable competitors. With greater risk, investors in the company's debt, preferred stock, and common stock would require higher returns. The cost of capital would be higher, the optimal financial leverage lower, and the value of the firm and its shareholders smaller.

Thus, the company's optimal capital structure is a function of prior company actions. In a more volatile economy with lower growth, the optimal proportion of debt in the capital structure would also be lower. A more stable environment would imply a higher financial leverage optimal.

Dividend Policy

Managers control the two key dividend policy decisions: the dividend payout rate and the dividend stability.

Dividend Payout. The **dividend payout rate** is the average proportion of earnings that are paid out (distributed) to common stockholders. The manager's objective is to obtain an appropriate long-run average payout rate. In FG the optimal long-run average payout ratio is a function of the growth rate of company earnings and the number and size of positive-NPV company investments.

The optimal payout rate is lower the higher the company's earnings growth rate and the higher the sum of investment NPVs. Conversely, mature companies in a nongrowth or negative-growth industry would have a very high optimal payout ratio, potentially exceeding total earnings.

In the real world—as in FG—the optimal payout rate is not obvious even though the preceding general rule on the payout rate holds. Managers in FG can best try to isolate the optimal payout rate or range by examining variations in payout rates across the set of companies participating in the game. Due to numerous other possible management and performance differences across companies, the ability to define an optimal payout range is possible, but difficult.

Optimal payout is inversely related to company growth opportunities. Certain dividends are more valuable than uncertain dividends.

Dividend Stability. A stable dividend policy exists when there are no decreases in the common stock cash dividend over time. A near-certain stream of dividends is viewed by risk-averse investors to be preferred to an uncertain stream. This is true since companies would be more likely to (1) cut dividends when the economy is doing poorly and (2) pay dividends when the economy is doing well. Dollars from dividends are more valuable to investors in poor times than in boom periods. Thus, an expected dollar of dividends received in every likely economic condition is more valuable than an expected dollar of dividends where no dollars are received when the economy is doing poorly and extra dollars are received when the economy is booming. FG investors follow this rule and find stable dividends more valuable than unstable dividends, all else equal. Managers may be constrained from achieving dividend stability due to the conditions of their industry.

Dividend stability is constrained by the company environment. Unit sales are not affected by the discount policy in FG.

  The amount of common stock cash dividends that can be paid out by any FG company that has debt and/or preferred stock is restricted. Commonly required by debt indentures (contracts) and preferred stockholder rights, real-world restrictions often exist on the amount of dividends that can be paid to common stockholders in poor economic times. These clauses and contractual conditions exist to protect debt holders and preferred stockholders. They would lose wealth if managers failed to satisfy their claims while giving liquidating dividends to common stockholders.

Other Interrelationships. Additional external funds will be needed over time if dividends increase. Cost of acquired funds could be affected. Stable dividends require cash outflows in even the worst of times, and additional external funds may be required in quarters when the cost of external funds is at its highest. Yet, if the company predicts sufficient future profitability and has capacity for more debt or equity, the dividend stability should be retained. Investors see the continued dividend level as a signal that the managers, with greater inside company information, foresee greater profitability. Likewise, a loss of dividend stability when dividends are decreased is a major negative signal indicating that the managers see protracted problems for the company. Large stock price decreases and wealth losses to shareholders then follow.

Discount on Receivables

In the real world, the discount policy can be used to induce customers to make cash payments rather than to buy goods on account. An equivalent alternative explanation is that the higher price required of credit sales provides the company a return for the additional funds invested in accounts receivable due to the granting of credit. Discount policies are often very similar or the same among all companies within specific industries in the real world. The offering of a discount policy can satisfy different customer clientele groups. Cash customers get a price concession while the company provides financing to customers desiring credit. Appropriate credit policies are thereby viewed as having the ability to increase sales, as often occurs with actual companies. In FG no unit sales changes are induced from the accounts receivable policy. Additionally, since sales are not affected by the discount policy, managers do not have to consider customer responses to changes in discount policy over time in FG. Given these conditions, the optimal discount policy in FG is both a simpler task and a less realistic portrayal than in an actual company.

  The effective cost (dollar discount) of a specific credit policy given in FG needs to be compared with the dollar decrease in the investment in accounts receivable to determine the cost of funds freed with the policy. The use of the next discount policy (0 to 1 percent, or 1 percent to 2 percent) is justified if funds are freed at a quarterly percent cost less than the quarterly percent cost of short-term loans. The pre-tax short-term loan rate is used since it has a similar maturity and risk as the cash flows from accounts receivable decreases. The short-term loan rate represents a more reasonable risk-adjusted discount (RAD) rate and investor opportunity cost than the firm's WACC.

Other Interrelationships. In FG the discount policy decision should be viewed as an alternative to short-term loans. A given discount policy is accepted if the effective cost of freed funds is less than short-term loans cost. The estimated period cash flows are impacted since large accounts receivable investment differences exist based on the discount policy adopted. Additionally, discounts are not viewed as a financial expense; they are directly subtracted from sales revenue in FG. Thus, financial expenses, debt interest coverage ratios, and financial leverage ratios would all be improved if the funds freed from a discount policy were used to reduce debt. Debt would be viewed as less risky and the costs of all sources of external funds would be less expensive. This set of conditions would most likely not hold in an actual company.

Production Strategy

The production strategy includes the management of inventory and both machine and plant capacity. An optimal strategy occurs when the last marginal dollar invested in a combination of inventory, machine capacity, and plant capacity required toward production of a unit of product provides sufficient return to cover the cost of capital and the next invested dollar does not cover this cost. Use a finance text to review the separate safety-stock and economic order quantity decision models. The models are appropriate for use for both inventory and productive capacity management.

Inventory.   The objective is to minimize the total cost of carrying inventory where total costs include both carrying and stock-out costs. In FG, carrying costs of inventory include the warehousing cost per unit and the cost of capital invested in carrying the unit. In the real world, additional carrying costs would include wastage, spoilage, pilferage, insurance, and technological obsolescence costs. Stock-out costs in FG include the after-tax profit forgone by having insufficient inventory to meet the sales demand. The marginal contribution provided by each unit sold is very high in FG. This means that per unit stock-out costs are also very high relative to the carrying cost per unit.

The **profit contribution** on a unit sold is equal to the sales price of the unit less all variable out-of-pocket costs. The expected value of the profit contribution is equal to the profit contribution times the likelihood that the unit will be sold. The planning requirements of managers include:

- Determine the carrying costs per unit at various inventory levels.
- Calculate the per unit stock-out cost.
- Find the inventory size where the expected per unit carrying costs plus the expected per unit stock-out costs are minimized. This is the optimal inventory subject to constraints covered later in this subsection.
- Provide sufficient productive capacity to, on average, maintain optimal inventory.

Machine and Plant Capacity.   Production in FG is limited to the lesser of machine or plant capacity. Investment in the next unit of both plant and machine capacity is justified if the expected value of the profit contribution is sufficient to cover depreciation and the cost of capital on the investment.

Example.   Adopt the assumption that hypothetically there is, on average, a 60 percent chance that the next unit will be sold in any given period. The average unit sales price over the life of the machine and plant is estimated at $100. The per unit effects follow: (1) The marginal materials and labor cost is $40. (2) The estimated marginal long-term selling and administrative costs total $15 (or $100 × 5% + [$1,000,000 fixed per period cost divided by a hypothetical optimal production level of 100,000]). (3) Warehousing fees are $3. (4) Long-run overhead is $2 (or $200,000 per period cost divided by the hypothetical optimal production level). The profit contribution is then $40 (or $100 − $40 − $15 − $3 − $2). The expected profit contribution is $24 (or 60% × $40). The unit of machinery costs $50; the unit of plant costs $325. The per period depreciation is $22.50 (or $50/8 + 325/20). As a rough proxy the average investment is $187.50 (or [$50 + $325] /2). The average quarterly cost of capital is 3 percent. The average cost of capital is $5.625 (or $187.5 × 3%). The expected per period loss on the next unit of plant and machinery purchased is estimated to be $4.125 (the expected contribution of $24 less the depreciation of $22.50 and cost of capital of $5.625). Expected costs exceed expected gains so the unit of capacity would not be added.

Long-run variable costs that are short-run fixed costs are included in the example based on getting sufficient revenues over time to cover all costs for a going concern. This represents an underlying going-concern-versus-abandonment decision. To cover the $2 overhead and $10 fixed selling and administrative cost, the presumption of a going concern is adopted in the preceding example. There is also an EOQ decision with plant additions. This condition occurs in FG because of a $250,000 order cost for every plant addition decision. Carrying costs in an FG plant EOQ decision include the cost of capital for holding the extra units of capacity and a wastage cost based on the depreciation on the units of plant attributable to periods when the units of plant will not be used due to a temporary excess capacity. Students need to use EOQ modeling from finance texts to determine the relative frequency and size of optimal plant additions. Optimal inventory, plant capacity, and machine capacity are interrelated.

With cyclical or variable demand over time, higher average inventory balances can be used to meet peak period unit demand. Lower capacity levels of machine and plant units are required to maintain the same overstocking and stock-out likelihood. The long-term strategy is to have the combination that maximizes the present value of future benefits less future costs.

Other Interrelationships.   The desirability of capital budgeting projects would be a function of the optimal production level. Higher levels would qualify more capital budgeting projects while lower production levels would decrease project acceptances. With greater investment in plant and equipment, the financing requirements increase; they decrease with less capacity. More external financing will be required the higher the optimal capacity level. The optimal dividend payout rate would likely decrease if greater value comes from capacity increases, while dividend increases would follow from optimal capacity decreases.

Unit Pricing Strategy

Managers have control over the unit sales price. If unit demand is elastic to price changes, the optimal pricing strategy is to reduce unit price below the price that holds in the market if the price is not controlled by the manager. Alternatively, the optimal pricing strategy is to increase unit price if demand is inelastic to price changes. Managers should consult a managerial economics book to understand the concepts and see how to measure the demand elasticity in FG. The more difficult decision is to then determine the optimal price change.

In FG the quarterly product sales demand is affected when manager's unit sales price differs from the underlying market clearing price. Yet, demand is not affected by the manager's prior pricing strategy or the product sales-pricing

Demand elasticity to price changes needs to be measured.

behavior of other firms. Managers have no direct way to differentiate their product by serving different markets or modifying product design.

Price Reductions.   The objective of this strategy is to increase unit sales, sales revenue, earnings, and common shareholder wealth. This last objective is often achieved by simultaneously lowering unit production cost and increasing unit demand. Lower unit production costs may result from economies of scale. The more elastic demand is to price decreases, the greater the unit demand increase and potential benefit from judicious price decreases from the otherwise underlying market equilibrium price. There is clearly a limit to the decrease in price that would maximize company value. As evidence, a unit price of zero per unit could ultimately lead to a company value of zero.

> **Example.**   In FG, the $1,000,000 fixed quarterly administrative cost leads to a lower per unit cost at higher unit production levels. Per unit profits thus increase at higher production levels. The NPV of A and B capital budgeting projects increase until their per quarter savings are maximized at production levels of 100,000 units for A and 120,000 units for B. Optimal safety stock investment levels for cash, inventory, and capacity levels all increase at a decreasing rate as the unit production level increases.

All three of the prior examples represent the phenomenon of increasing economies of scale. A diseconomy of scale occurs beyond 120,000 unit production due to increasing per unit labor costs.

Lower price generates additional product demand. Total profits and performance are increased if the profits from more units sold exceed the losses from a likely reduction in the profit margin with a lower sales price. In a successful price reduction strategy, there must be an expected positive marginal profit from the unit sales gain. Symbolically,

$$(P_1 - C_1)\, Q_1 > (P_0 - C_0)\, Q_0 \qquad (3.1)$$

where

P = Price per unit of output
C = Cost per unit
Q = Quantity of units sold

The subscript 0 indicates before, and 1 is after the price reduction.

The new expected quantity (Q_1), price (P_1), and cost (C_1) are long-run expected values, not necessarily the initial quantity, price, and cost required to get to the new permanent expected quantity, Q_1. Temporary differences in optimal inventory levels, plant capacity, machine capacity, and capital budgeting projects selected might result in a temporary price per unit that is different from the long-run P_1 and a temporary quantity demanded that is different from the long-run permanent expected quantity demand of Q_1.

Managers must seek information on the impact of company-initiated price decreases on sales demand when judging revenue changes. Likewise, the costs per unit associated with generating the additional sales need to be derived. Equation 3.1 is used to judge whether the strategy of reducing unit price is sound.

Other Interrelationships.   Higher volume will increase the optimal relative plant and machine capacity. Marginally lower implied stock-out costs associated with the smaller forgone per unit profit contribution might lead to lower relative

Management lowering of unit price leads to unit demand increases and profit margin decreases. Managers must first measure the reaction to price changes to determine the optimal direction of price change.

inventory levels. This is offset by the higher average demand level that would require a higher optimal investment in inventory. The desirability of capital budgeting projects would typically be increased because of higher volume production and an increase in the expected total labor savings per project.

With greater investment in plant and equipment, the financing requirements increase. More external financing will be required. The smaller profit margin per unit decreases the potential benefit from increased volume sales generated by greater advertising costs.

Price Increases.   The same evaluation procedure just covered with price decreases can be used in judging whether a price increase above the industry-specified price is justified. Planning differences consistent with a higher-price and lower-volume objective are potentially numerous.

If a price increase is optimal, there will be offsetting reductions due to the loss of economies of scale discussed under the preceding price-decrease section. Per unit profit margin will increase. The extra profits from the greater contribution margin per unit will have to offset the profit forgone on the incremental unit sales lost with the price increase. Again, Equation 3.1 should be used to estimate long-run earnings impacts.

Other Interrelationships.   Lower volume will reduce the optimal plant and machine capacities. Higher implied stock-out costs associated with the greater forgone per unit profit contribution might lead to higher relative inventory levels. Offsetting this, the lower expected sales volume reduces the optimal inventory safety-stock size. The desirability of capital budgeting projects would typically be reduced because of lower-volume production and a reduction in total labor savings per project. With less investment in plant and equipment, the financing requirements decrease. The larger profit margin per unit increases the potential benefit from increased sales volume generated by greater advertising costs.

Warning: There is a limit on how much of a price increase or decrease is optimal if the industry-determined price is suboptimal. An infinite unit demand at a price of zero surely cannot maximize profits. So, too, a sales price of $999.99 per unit with no units demanded is not profitable and won't maximize investor wealth. By default, the maintenance of the market equilibrium price is optimal if neither the price increase nor decrease from the industry level leads to increased expected profits in Equation 3.1.

In review, the two pricing strategies should help the FG manager realize that the adopted strategy will affect productive capacity, product pricing, inventory policy, capital budgeting decisions, and thereby the mix and level of external versus internal financing requirements. Profitability, volatility of profitability, and cash flows are all influenced by the selected strategy. In turn, shareholder accumulated wealth is affected.

So many variables are affected by the pricing strategy that many inept managers fail to do the necessary learning, investigative work, measurement, planning, and analysis to determine the optimal pricing strategy. Shareholders quickly realize the inadequacy of their managers relative to the optimal pricing companies that are maximizing their common stockholders' accumulated wealth, and the company's stock price drops accordingly.

A common suboptimal or "second-best" pricing policy uses price to manage temporary shortages of capacity or excess inventory balances. Under this scenario, if managers see a capacity shortage in the next period, they increase price to decrease demand, increase profit margin per unit, and improve the relative position of their company had they not controlled product unit price. If they have excess inventory estimated for the next period, they decrease price, increase demand, and work down their excess inventory. Shareholder accumulated wealth can be increased with these policies. The increase is considerably less than that achieved with the more appropriate management policy covered next.

An increased contribution margin must offset higher unit costs and reduced unit sales.

A Possible Method of Attack. A manager can follow the steps below in establishing pricing strategy.

- As soon as managers receive control over the unit price, they should seek information on the impact of using a unit sales price that is different from the unit price that occurs with no management control.
- Since the impact of a price change is unknown, a small price change from the price that would occur without management control is initiated.
- The pricing chapter or section of a managerial economics book needs to be reviewed to determine price–demand relationships and the measurement of demand elasticity to price changes.
- Managers measure the demand elasticity to price changes for their company using the information from their above test of unit price impact.
- With the demand elasticity measured, a schedule of unit prices and the expected demand level for each price is constructed.
- A set of pro forma statements is prepared for each of the different price–demand pairs.
- The marginal return on investment to go to the next lower price is measured. This is achieved by finding the difference in earnings divided by the difference in investment of two adjacent sets of price–demand pairs from the above schedule.
- As a rough rule, if the return on additional investment is less than the cost of capital, the next higher price set of adjacent pairs of demand and price needs examination. If the return on investment is greater than the cost of capital, the next lower price set of adjacent pairs needs examination.
- The prior step is replicated until:
  1. Capacity limits are reached, or
  2. If successively lower prices have been examined and the prior return on investments is greater than the cost of capital and the current return on investment is lower than the cost of capital, select the prior pair of demand and price levels, or
  3. If successively higher prices have been examined and the prior return on investments is less than the cost of capital and the current return on investment is greater than the cost of capital, select the prior pair of demand and price levels.

The above procedure provides a crude estimate of the temporary optimal manager-determined price. The plant capacity, machine capacity, and capital budgeting investment level have not yet been adjusted to determine the long-run optimal unit pricing strategy. The above procedure would at least move the company toward the long-term optimal strategy.

At the long-term optimal pricing point, the long-run variable out-of-pocket cost required to generate a unit, including cost of the capital invested to generate a unit of production capacity and sales, equals the per unit sales price.

Advertising

A manager's advertising decision impacts a company's product demand. The only impact from advertising in FG is to increase product demand in the quarter that the advertising expense is incurred. The objective would be to determine the level of advertising that maximizes profits.

The decision on advertising is more complex if the manager also controls unit pricing. Both of these variables and the underlying elasticity of demand to price changes all simultaneously determine the unit demand. Further, both unit pricing and advertising can change the level of the elasticity of demand to price. The relative impact of the joint use of the two decisions on unit demand is also affected by the strength of the economy. Thereby, the optimal company unit capacity and output level may change with advertising expenditures. Depending on the above conditions, further testing and analysis are required if the manager has control of advertising. The limited number of periods of play in FG may be insufficient to determine the optimal combinations of unit pricing and advertising. Yet, the manager can be moving toward greater profitability and shareholder wealth with sound planning during this time.

As with unit price of product, the objective is to derive the long-term optimal advertising level. Suboptimal use of advertising holds if managers use advertising to temporarily adjust demand upward when the company is short on capacity. The optimal advertising level can be determined only with testing the consequences of advertising. The objective is to increase advertising if the marginal advertising dollar results in a marginal earnings increase that at least covers the additional cost of capital on the investment required in meeting the advertising-induced expanded sales. In FG, a floor level of advertising may be needed to induce any positive sales impact. At a sufficiently high level of advertising, each successive dollar of advertising has less of a marginal benefit.

As with unit price of product, the short-term consequences are often different from the long-term consequences. For example, long-run capacity levels are variable, while they are fixed in the short run. Thus, a short-term advertising optimal would be determined subject to inventory and capacity levels. In the longer-term perspective, the inventory and capacity levels are variable-cost components that need to be included in determining if the marginal dollar of advertising generates sufficient revenue to cover all costs.

Other Interrelationships.   Marginally higher stock-out costs associated with the higher forgone per unit profit contribution might lead to higher inventory levels. This higher inventory size is reinforced by the higher average demand level that would require a higher optimal investment in inventory. The desirability of capital budgeting projects would typically be increased because of higher-volume production and an increase in the expected total labor savings per project. With greater investment in plant and equipment, the financing requirements increase. More external financing might be required.

Integrating the Set of Decisions

The consequences of individual and subsets of decisions controlled by the manager go beyond the direct effects of the decisions described earlier in the chapter. To obtain a better feel for the integration requirements coming from control of all the manager decisions, all of the "Other Interrelationships" subsections earlier in the chapter should now be reexamined before proceeding.

The extensive sets of interrelationships just reviewed indicate the complex environment in which the manager must make large numbers of interrelated decisions. Numerous decisions are required at each point in time (quarterly in FG) that will have both temporary and permanent consequences on the position and performance of the company.

The development of a strategy should have multiple stages. Here is one possible method of attack:

- Review the theory, models, and solution procedures for individual decision management discussed in finance and managerial economics texts. This includes management of each decision subarea covered earlier in the chapter.
- Using text information and the information from each decision area in the chapter, do the necessary analysis to make a preliminary decision on each decision item.
  1. Capital budgeting decisions should be made since the manager has the required information for an informed decision. This includes generating a cost-of-capital estimate and deriving NPVs on both current quarterly projects A and B. Positive NPV projects are accepted.
  2. Preliminary decisions still must be made that rely on forecasts whose accuracy are unknown. Insufficient and unreliable information does not enable the manager to yet determine if these are optimal decisions. These include:
     a. Unit price of product.
     b. Purchase of demand and price forecast.
     c. Plant and machine capacity additions.
     d. Sales discount on receivables.
     e. Common stock dividend.
- Avoid the external financing of needed investments with the set of decisions used to determine the first pro forma set of statements for the next quarter. The marketable securities balance sheet balance for the quarter just completed should also be eliminated by a negative entry on the "Short-term investment" decision for next quarter's first pro forma set of decisions. This is done since the end-of-quarter liquidity position has not yet been determined and marketable securities should initially be viewed as surplus cash.
- Create a set of pro forma statements using the decisions derived above. From the quarterly position statement (balance sheet) subtract the penalty loan balance from the cash balance to determine the ending cash surplus (positive balance) or ending cash shortage (negative balance).
- Determine the temporary cash surplus or shortage by subtracting a cash safety stock buffer from the number just derived.
- Obtain external financing to cover any cash shortage. The manager's initial strategy on optimal capital structure and the target maturity mix of debt is

used to determine the sources of the needed financing. If the target capital structure has changed from the initial decisions and/or the estimated cost of capital has changed, the NPVs of A and B may need to be revised. The sources of funding selected should be consistent with maintaining the initial long-term financing strategy.

- If surplus funds exist, decide either to temporarily store the funds in marketable securities or to retire securities. If the funds are not expected to be needed in the next quarter, most of the marketable securities should be retired since the savings in the cost of capital will heavily outweigh the interest that could be earned.
- Based on the above, make decision entries regarding
  1. Short-term or marketable securities investment.
  2. Short-term loans.
  3. Two-year loans.
  4. Three-year loans.
  5. Long-term loans.
  6. Preferred stock.
  7. Common stock.
  8. Modifying the acceptance decisions on A and B if NPVs have changed sign.
- If item 8 has changed, return to "Create a set of pro forma statements. . ." and replicate the remaining steps. This process is repeated until the necessary financing is in place to generate the desired end-of-period cash safety-stock target balance.

The above process is needed each quarter to:

- Maintain liquidity.
- Implement and finance desirable capital budgeting projects.
- Maintain the company's dividend policy and basic production requirements.
- Seek information on the management-controlled decisions where more information is needed before being able to derive an optimal decision in the future.

The capable manager continues to seek the necessary information to determine the direction, if not the location, of an optimal policy on a given decision variable. As the manager moves the company toward this policy, the consequences (interrelationships) with other decisions must be considered. These other decisions may need adjustments to accommodate the revised strategy of the company. Consequences flow in both directions. The optimal location of the new decision may change as the other variables controlled by the manager are adjusted to accommodate the new decision.

> **Example.**   Adopt the assumption that the optimal pricing strategy is to decrease unit price because demand is price-elastic. Optimal plant capacity, machine capacity, and inventory levels all increase. This requires greater demand for external funds, which will probably increase the cost of capital. The secondary consequence of the cost of capital increase is to decrease the optimal unit price, plant capacity, machine capacity, and optimal investment level in all other assets.

The strategy is by nature an adaptive one where new information is received each quarter. The manager must respond to the new information. The manager's response may need to run the range of possible changes from none to a major revision in strategy, possibly requiring the abandonment of part or all of the company's prior strategy.

Company Life Cycle

The optimal mixes of ingredients needed for firms in different stages of maturity are not the same. Optimal financial mix is strongly dependent on the life cycle position of a company.

Four dimensions of the financing strategy are affected by a company's maturity:

- New or declining firms have a more costly set of financing sources than an established or mature company.
- The proportion of internally versus externally generated funds increases with company maturity.
- The amount of investment per period as a percentage of total assets decreases as the company becomes more mature.
- Higher growth rate and younger firms have less financial leverage, proportionally more equity and less debt than lower growth and larger firms.

New companies and companies in declining industries find acquisition of long-term debt financing to be more costly (if it is available at all) than do mature non-declining companies. Potential creditors view the risks to be higher for firms with lower and less certain cash flows and less real collateral; the likelihood of satisfying loan principal and interest payments is lower. For the riskier firms in the real world, long-term debt either is not available or is available only when substantial risk premiums are included in the debt interest rate. In FG, no restrictions on the methods of financing exist based on company life cycle, although many limits on management hold for financially troubled firms.

New Companies

New, growing companies often have an insatiable demand for new funds. The unsatisfied appetite comes from high project net present values and the resulting windfall gains for equity holders. Even with high profitability, the growth in investment in all asset accounts on the balance sheet outdistances the company's internal generation of funds. Profits and cash inflows from operations are insufficient to meet the demand for more investable funds.

A large proportion of the funds invested has to come from external sources. These external equity sources of funds are often restricted for new companies. The potential dilution in both future earnings growth and original owner-manager control often leads to an objective of minimizing common stock offerings. With new high-growth firms, potential and expected future windfall gains come from most investments since they have large positive net present values. If external investors do not foresee these truly available windfalls, new shares will be underpriced. These publicly unrecognized windfalls must then be shared with any new common equity holders, lowering the expected wealth gains of the original investors. This condition is one source of what is called *the agency cost of equity*. The agency cost holds when equity is issued for less than its fair value, leading to an increased cost of common stock. Thereby, the WACC also increases and the company underinvests since there are projects it would have adopted that now have a negative NPV.

Due to this condition, most or all internally generated funds are reinvested in the company and no dividends are paid to common shareholders. High financial leverage is also generally not desirable due to the greater uncertainty on future cash flows of high growth and newer companies. Higher levels of financial leverage are also avoided since debtholders generally place many controls and constraints on a company and its future financing options and speed. This hampers the flexibility of a new and high-growth company to make timely and appropriate decisions in its rapidly changing environment.

Mature and Declining Companies

Firms in declining (negative-growth) industries face their own unique problems that affect policy formation. Declining firms are in the process of liquidation. Internal generation of funds exceeds the need for investment funds for profitable firms in their declining phase. The firm either invests the excess "cash throw-off" in other lines of business or follows an orderly process of planned liquidation. Cash inflows first go to the line of business investments that provide an adequate return. Any remaining cash balances that cannot be invested to get a positive NPV are used to reduce both debt and equity claims. This last alternative is available in FG. The ability to invest in other lines of business is not available in FG.

Mature and declining companies are mismanaged if excess funds that cannot be reinvested to earn an adequate return are retained in the company. This phenomenon is referred to as an *excess free cash flow problem*. Permanent marketable security balances and excess cash balances thus represent poor management in both FG and actual companies.

Equity claims are usually reduced by either fairly large cash dividends or repurchases of company stock in open market transactions. Debt claims are commonly reduced by first paying off maturing debt obligations and then retiring debt before maturity. The need for refinancing is limited since the firm is in the process of liquidating. Again, the financial strategy reflects the life cycle position of the company. The stage of the life cycle and tax consequences have led profitable declining firms to a specific exit strategy where there is an optimal dividend policy, investment policy, planned phased withdrawal from unprofitable businesses, and an exit strategy. Withdrawal from a section of the business would be based on the best wealth maximizing or conserving alternative including spin-offs, sell-offs, and split-offs if the business component has sufficient going concern value and liquidation if the abandonment value exceeds going concern value.

More mature firms with average growth rates might still have a moderately high dividend payout rate. Some in finance believe that dividends should be paid even if this requires managers to occasionally go to capital markets to issue new common stock. The requirement to get external equity funds serves as a monitoring function on managers. In this setting, external equity providers serve as judge and jury through their pricing of the company's new shares. They attest to whether managers have or have not acted in the past in the best interest of external (non-management) equity holders.

Life Cycle Impacts on Overall Strategy

Financial strategy in FG should be formulated with a recognition of the impact of company life cycle on appropriate management of the set of company decisions.

Over the quarters of the game, the instructor can select production levels and product prices that impose a specific life cycle position on FG companies. The company can have high growth, moderate growth, no growth, or negative growth over your tenure as manager.

The level of profitability for each possible growth option can be changed. A manager may be burdened with an unprofitable declining firm. The best manager in this environment would be the first to recognize, plan, and initiate an orderly liquidation of the company.

At the other extreme, the company could have a high growth rate and be very profitable. The best manager would be the first to recognize, plan, and initiate investment policies for plant, machine, capital budgeting, financing, and dividends that are consistent with a high-growth environment. A proper financial strategy would leave the firm neither too financially leveraged nor with too much equity.

The instructor may choose to tell the managers the life cycle position of companies in the industry. Most instructors leave it to the managers to both determine their firm's life cycle position and develop optimal investment and financial strategies consistent with their environment.

Managers' Risk-Bearing Tolerance

The propensity of a manager to take risks to attain higher expected returns directly influences the company's selected overall strategy. Product marketing strategy, risk in investment decisions, and financial strategy are all partially determined by the manager's attitude toward risk taking or risk avoidance. Looking at extreme risk positions and a moderate risk position, we gain insight into how manager preferences influence the formation of a strategy.

Risk Bearing in Actual Companies

Risk-Taking Managers.   Managers with a style incorporating high levels of risk taking are called innovators, daring, imaginative, flamboyant, and even geniuses—if their dreams come true. The energy and spirit of the manager drive the organization toward goals that most people would be too meek to attempt. Product innovation, vertical and horizontal product integration, high financial leverage, and widespread use of hybrid securities are typical of the resulting company strategy.

A high-risk approach can be dangerous. One serious error, like incorrectly estimating a downturn in the economy, can be sufficient to threaten a firm's existence. The prior gains of numerous successful chance decisions can be lost with one unsuccessful decision. Sometimes incorrectly, the previous genius can now be called reckless, inconsistent, flighty, or even a charlatan.

Risk-Averse Managers.   At the opposite end of the continuum are the conservative managers who attempt to avoid risk at almost any cost. Product innovation is low. Debt is often viewed as being as bad as the plague. Cash balances and the amount of marketable securities are commonly excessive. Investors are generally rewarded with large dividend yields since security price appreciation is fairly low and for obvious reasons not anticipated in the future. Companies in this category make excellent acquisition candidates for the risk-taking companies. Excess assets can be liquidated and financial leverage increased after acquisition to provide large cash inflows to the acquiring company. The positive cash flow enables still further acquisitions or the direct purchase of assets to further aid the growth of the riskier company. Unlike the real world, mismanaged companies cannot be bought out in FG.

Middle-of-the-Road Managers.   The continuum between the highly leveraged and the very conservative managers contains what can be called the "average" manager. A specific manager may have a mix of goals that in some areas represent high risk preference and in others high risk aversion. The firm might be high on product innovation and low on financial leverage. Opposite risk positions represent a counterbalancing of opposing forces and not necessarily a set of inconsistent goals. The manager's area of expertise, personnel preferences, and attitudes toward specific policy options are reflected in the overall adopted company strategy. A new manager will impose a different set of values and standards in modifying the company strategy to best reflect his or her talents and preferences.

Managers' Risk Tolerance in FinGame

The FG manager brings knowledge, attitudes, and preferences to the game. Conservative or liberal positions can be taken with production and inventory policy, financial leverage, and dividend policies. A liberal production policy could be indicated by higher capacity and commitments to higher fixed charges. Higher future sales levels could be motivated through both the control of the product price and larger quantity purchases of capacity additions when prices are low. Lower costs per unit and higher-volume sales could lead to greater profitability and performance. Higher risks come from the possibility that the new capacity might not be utilized and would burden the firm with higher unavoidable fixed costs.

Conservative managers wait for verification of permanent increases in demand before adding capacity. Possible higher costs of capacity additions and opportunity losses from forgone profits on missed sales are potential costs of this production strategy.

Inventory stockpiling based on an uncertain future sales demand exceeding production capacity may be safer, but very costly. Failure of the uncertain sales demand to meet expectations leads to large multiple-period inventory carrying costs and necessitates future production cuts that increase the per unit product costs. Both the higher carrying costs and the production costs per unit narrow the contribution margin and company earnings. A tight inventory policy increases the probability of stock-out costs and possible lower relative earnings. A just-in-time inventory policy could be very costly in FG due to the high per unit stock-out costs and uncertain demand.

A conservative financial leverage policy reduces the risk of downside earnings and losses when industry sales decline while concurrently reducing the expected earnings per share to stockholders. Managers must determine to what extent financial leverage can be used to improve shareholders' wealth. Liberal managers clearly maintain the belief that large amounts of debt in the capital structure are best for shareholders' wealth. If their financial leverage is excessive, they will not maximize common stockholders' accumulated wealth.

A conservative dividend policy would include stable dividends and a fairly high payout rate relative to other companies in the same industry. Whether this policy is optimal depends on the opportunities the company has for investing funds to earn an adequate or more than adequate return. Managers of a company with low payout and lack of stability perceive returns from the reinvestment of funds to be sufficient to justify a low priority for cash dividends.

Due to differences in the patterns of unit demand and unit price that can exist in the FG environment, anything from a very conservative to a very liberal overall management strategy may be optimal. A very stable time series of demands and unit prices would indicate an ability, on average, for the liberal manager to perform better. A very cyclical time series would probably be consistent with a more conservative overall strategy being optimal.

The capable manager is responsive to the environment and adopts an alternative strategy in light of new information. The manager might have taken an appropriate liberal approach to financial leverage due to initial evidence of a high-growth company. Immediate action to revise the financial leverage downward would be required if new information indicates that the previously perceived high growth was only a cyclical upturn that was now reversing.

Conclusion

As in the real world, the capable manager will formulate a plan of action, or strategy, that realistically recognizes the company's environment. Both variables outside of manager control and external constraints on the range of management decisions must be considered in establishing a viable strategy.

Implementation of a possible strategy is evaluated by estimating the consequences of the strategy on company position and performance. Sets of pro forma financial statements are constructed based on decisions that come from the envisioned company strategy. The decisions are then implemented if the estimated results from the pro forma statements are sufficiently consistent with managers' expectations of strategy impact.

A modified strategy and new pro forma statements that follow from this modification are required if the estimated impact of the original strategy is unacceptable. Quite often managers experiment with new possible strategies by estimating their impact on future financial statements. The old (or current) strategy is abandoned when a new strategy is found that is expected to increase shareholder wealth. This same adaptive managerial approach to modifying the company plan is appropriate for the FG company manager.

The Company Environment and Rules

Overview

This chapter looks at rules and conditions defining the company gaming environment. The first section discusses the mechanics of operating the company. The second section serves as the primary reference source to be used throughout the game. An alphabetized cross reference to all rules is provided in the chapter Appendix.

Company Management Instructions

Company operating instructions and rules must be understood for successful management.

The following conditions are critical to sound management of a new FG company:

- The first reading of the rules will introduce the manager to the scope of the FG decision environment.
- Repeated review of the rules and conditions in this chapter will be necessary. The rules pertaining to a given decision should be scrutinized before each period of play. The game does not require memorization of the rules. A thorough understanding of the direct and indirect financial and operational consequences of decisions is critical in competently managing any firm, whether in finance or human relations or in FinGame or General Electric.
- Each time a new decision is made, the rules and conditions related to the decision need to be evaluated in detail. Just as a chef cannot make a soufflé with no knowledge of the ingredients and proportions, the method of combining ingredients, the cooking time and temperature, an FG manager cannot run a complex business by guesses and with limited to no information. In FG, the company's performance will indicate the manager's competence in understanding how decisions affect the company.
- To avoid misconceptions and unsound decisions, the manager should physically check off each point after determining the consequences of the rule on the company's financial plan.
- Because the manager makes irreversible decisions every quarter, a clerical error often irreparably harms a company for the rest of the game. Be careful! **Check all decisions!** In almost every class using FG, at least one

company will fail to produce units and another will not enter planned and required external financing to avoid large and expensive penalty loans. In a real business this would represent gross negligence.

- Chapters 1 through 4 *must* be read before a decision on the first quarter of management operation should be entered. *The first management decisions are required for quarter 2.* The company is created in quarter 1 and the starting financial statements are generated at the *end* of quarter 1.

- Some instructors may require students to prepare their own sets of budgeted, or pro forma, statements for the first quarter or few quarters of the game. The first set would be for quarter 2. Students would then be "locked out" from using the FG-generated pro forma statements. If student preparation of statements is required, a downloadable pdf file is available from the registered FG main menu page through a "Supplemental Materials" option called "Financial Statement Construction." This will need to be read before pro forma statements are prepared.

- The company's first set of financial statements for quarter 1 includes the quarterly Performance Report shown in Exhibit 4.1, the Position Statement in Exhibit 4.2, and the Summary Sheet of Exhibit 4.3. The instructor will notify FG managers if their companies have a different set of quarter 1 statements. If so, the starting statements will be generated by printing the modified quarter 1 statements after running the simulation for quarter 1, as noted in Chapter 2.

Note: Minor differences in numbers throughout Exhibits 4.1, 4.2, and 4.3 may be found with the actual quarter 1 simulation. Very material differences can occur when the instructor changes environmental conditions, such as the tax rate. Additionally, many of the forecasts in the Summary Sheet are estimates of what will occur during the actual quarter simulation. Differences between pro forma statement numbers and the actual statement numbers will represent these forecast errors. Commission and omission errors can also cause additional differences between pro forma statement numbers and the actual quarterly statements. For example, a failure to adjust interest rates appropriately for large debt offerings would represent a financial planning omission error.

- Unless stated otherwise by the instructor, the manager has control of all the decision variables available to the firm.

To prepare and use this game, the following five steps are required.

Step 1. The instructor will indicate which, if any, variables the manager will not control. The instructor will indicate the value for any decision not controlled by the participant.

Step 2. With the set of financial statements and the information in Chapters 3 and 4, the manager will come to a decision on all the controlled company decision variables.

Step 3. For example, in quarter 1, the controlled decisions for quarter 2 will be entered in the appropriate location of a **Pro Forma Decision Sheet for Quarter 2** (see Screen 3, Chapter 2) and simulated with the "Run Pro Forma Simulation" option if managers have the ability to use the FG pro forma statement generator. If the generator is not available, the manager must use the "Financial Statement Construction" pdf, available on the FG web site, as a guide in preparing pro forma statements by hand.

Step 4. The pro forma statements, viewable with the "View Pro Forma Results" option, need to be analyzed to see if common stockholders' objective of wealth maximization (see Chapter 3) is being achieved. If the objective is not being achieved, steps 3 and 4 will have to be redone with a new set of decisions.

Example. If the pro forma statements contain a sizable cash deficit represented by a large penalty loan, the manager has not secured sufficient external funds for the current quarter's planned expenditures. The plan has to be revised by increasing external funds and/or reducing investment from the original plan. A new set of pro forma statements from step 3 is then needed to see if the desired liquidity position has been achieved with the revised set of decisions.

Step 5. The actual quarterly decisions are entered (see Chapter 2) and the *irreversible* simulation of the next quarter is completed. A new set of financial reports and summary information, similar to Exhibits 4.1, 4.2, and 4.3, will be generated for the quarter just completed. Steps 1 through 5 are repeated for each period of play.

Company Operating Rules

The external environment in which the firm operates, along with the rules and conditions that form the internal company environment, is presented in this section. An explanation is given for each item in the set of financial statements (Exhibits 4.1, 4.2, and 4.3). Rules governing each possible management decision are also provided in detail.

The Industry Environment

The following characteristics hold for all FG companies:

- The firm produces and sells one undifferentiated and undefined product.
- All firms start the game with the same asset mix, financial structure, and potential for success.
- The firms in the game do not interact; that is, the decisions and the performance position of any one firm do not affect any other firm. This condition is consistent with the efficient markets hypothesis and competitive finance markets where one company's actions do not affect material changes over the entire financial market.
- A quarter of a year is the time increment for each period of play. This enables the possible inclusion of seasonal, cyclical, and secular trends in the demand for the company's output.
- Demand, product price, interest rates, and plant and machine costs are all affected by the general business conditions represented in the game by an economic indicator. Managers must determine the economic indicator's effect on the different variables. This knowledge needs to be incorporated into the firm's planning and decisions.
- Decisions are made in a condition of uncertainty. For example, the forecasts of demand and price are randomly distributed about the actual value. The player will not know the actual values; thus, a strategy for estimating the values is needed.

EXHIBIT 4.1

Company Name
Quarterly Performance Report
Quarter 1

Sales Revenue (97,383 units at 100.00)			$9,738,300
Income from Securities			2,725	$9,741,025
Cost of Goods Sold:			
Beginning Inventory: (9,809 at $74.79)			$ 733,567
Materials	$1,500,000		
Direct Labor	3,500,000		
Total Direct Costs		$ 5,000,000	
Warehousing Costs	$ 60,408		
Depreciation: Mach. and Equip.	478,125		
Plant	1,300,000		
Other Overhead Costs	200,000		
Total Indirect Costs		2,038,533	
Production Costs (100,000 at $70.39)			7,038,533
Goods Available for Sale (70.78 *per unit*)			7,772,100
Less: Ending Inventory (12,426 *units*)			879,492
Cost of Goods Sold				6,892,608
Gross Profit				$2,848,417
Selling and Administrative Expenses			$1,486,915
Financial Expenses:			
Short-Term Bank Interest		$ 0	
Penalty-Loan Interest		0	
Intermediate-Term Loan Interest		92,749	
Bond Interest		33,600	
Bond Redemption Costs		0	
Total Financial Charges			126,349	1,613,264
Operating Income before Extraordinary Items				$1,235,153
Extraordinary Items				0
Income before Taxes				$1,235,153
Income Tax (*rate is* 40%)				494,060
Income after Taxes				$ 741,093
Preferred Stock Dividend				0
Earnings to Common Stockholders				$ 741,093
Common Stock Dividends ($0.10 *per share*)				100,000
Net Income Transferred to Retained Earnings				$ 641,093

Operation of the Company

In this subsection, the rules covering revenues are provided first, followed by the rules affecting costs. The order of presentation of the rules is consistent with the process used to generate budgeted or pro forma financial statements. Each period, the managers are provided with the following:

1. A Performance Report (or income statement) following the format of Exhibit 4.1.
2. A Position Statement (or balance sheet) similar to Exhibit 4.2.
3. A Summary Sheet structured like Exhibit 4.3.

Information concerning past performance and the current position of the firm is given along with forecast information for future quarters. Exhibits 4.1, 4.2, and

EXHIBIT **4.2**

Company Name
Position Statement
Quarter 1

Assets

Current Assets		
Cash	$ 120,636	
Marketable Securities	200,000	
Accounts Receivable	6,524,661	
Inventory (12,426 *units at $70.78/Unit*)	879,492	
Total Current Assets		$ 7,724,789
Fixed Assets (*net of depreciation*)		
Machinery and Equipment	$ 2,008,125	
Plant	$ 7,165,250	
Total Fixed Assets		$ 9,173,375
Total Assets		$16,898,164

Liabilities and Owner Equity

Current Liabilities		
Accounts Payable	$ 520,000	
Short-Term Loans Payable	0	
Short-Term Penalty Loan	0	
Intermediate-Term Debt Maturing	1,850,000	
Bonds Maturing	$ 1,200,000	
Total Current Liabilities		$ 3,570,000
Long-Term Liabilities		
Intermediate Loans: 2 years	$ 937,500	
3 years	0	
Bonds	1,200,000	
Total Long-Term Liabilities		2,137,500
Total Liabilities		$5,707,500
Owners' Equity		
Preferred Stock (0 *shares*)	$ 0	
Common Stock (1,000,000 *shares*)	$8,000,000	
Retained Earnings	$3,190,664	
Total Equity		11,190,664
Total Liabilities and Equity		$16,898,164

4.3 indicate the firm's starting position at quarter 1 (unless modified by the instructor).

Revenues

Income is generated from both sales of the product and revenues from short-term investments. Sales of the product provide the major source of revenue. Short-term investments are most often used for temporary investment of excess cash.

Product Sales Estimation

Estimates of both the market's demand for the company's product and the price the market will pay per-unit demanded for each of the next four quarters are provided in the Summary Sheet. (See Exhibit 4.3 for estimates for quarters 2 through 5.)

EXHIBIT 4.3

Company Name
Summary Data—Quarter 1

Historical Information:

Common share price	$35.57	Accumulated wealth	$35.67
Quarterly EPS	0.74	Dividend yield	1.10%
Price-earnings ratio	12.00	Marketable security yield	1.362%
Actual unit price	100.00	Actual unit demand	97,383
Preferred stock price	32.15	Preferred dividend yield	3.11
Return on investment	17.54	Return on equity	26.49
Call premium: preferred	8.00%	Bond call premium	8.00%
Common tender or sell/sh	$0.00	Unpaid preferred dividend/share	$0.00

Outstanding debt yields:

Short-term	2-year loan	3-year loan	Bonds	Penalty loan
2.980%	3.110%	2.500%	1.400%	8.000%

Information for Future Quarters:

Quarter	2	3	4	5
Units forecast	105,721	103,295	123,736	117,871
Price per unit forecast	$ 99.81	$ 103.73	$ 103.03	$ 102.85
Units of plant capacity	100,000	100,000	100,000	80,000
Units of machine capacity	100,000	100,000	75,000	60,000
Other overhead	200,000	200,000	200,000	200,000
Depreciation:				
Machinery	478,125	478,125	384,375	311,250
Projects	0	0	0	0
Plant	1,300,000	1,300,000	1,300,000	989,000
Principal repayment on debt:				
Short-term	0	0	0	
2-year	312,500	312,500	312,500	312,500
3-year	300,000	300,000	0	0
Bonds	300,000	300,000	300,000	300,000
Warehouse fees:				
Units		First 2000	Next 5000	Over 7000
Cost/Unit		$ 1.00	$ 3.00	$ 8.00

Production costs per unit next quarter:

Materials	$15.00 Machinery	$47.00	Plant	$321.00
Units	First 60,000	Next 40,000	Next 20,000	Over 120,000
Labor cost	$39.00	$29.00	$25.00	$33.00

Rates on funding in quarter 2

Short-term	2-year loan	3-year loan	Bond	Preferred
1.981%	1.915%	1.854%	1.754%	2.620%

Interest due next quarter:

Short-term	$ 0
Intermediate	$83,030
Bonds	$33,600

Capital budgeting projects for next quarter:

	Life	Cost	Unit Capacity	Overhead Saving	Unit Labor Sav., Qtr. 2	Change/Qtr. Labor Sav.
A	2-yr	$659,280	100,000	$15,340	$0.82	$0.03
B	3-yr	$513,432	120,000	−$8,102	$0.85	−$0.01

EXHIBIT 4.4   **Generation of Demand Estimates**

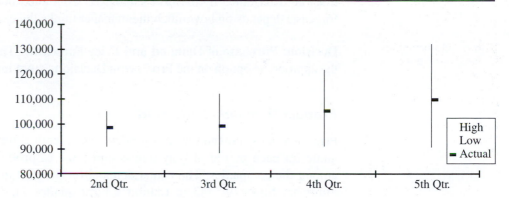

Estimates for more recent quarters are more accurate than estimates for more distant quarters. In Exhibit 4.4, the vertical lines provide a hypothetical range of the possible forecasts of quarterly demand. The estimates are uniformly distributed along the hypothetical range lines. An independent new set of estimates is generated each quarter. Thus, by the end of quarter 4, there will be a total of four estimates for quarter 5 demand (and price), one from each quarter's output 1 through 4.

More recent demand and sales price estimates are most accurate.

Manager Objective.   The manager has little information at the start of the game and must develop a strategy for both securing and evaluating information. The accuracy of the price and demand estimates can be evaluated only after several periods of play by comparing previous estimates with actual outcomes. As the game progresses, greater reliance can be placed on the accuracy of the estimates. The forecast demand and price estimates are needed to make decisions on production levels, needed machine and plant capacity, and funding requirements.

Purchase of Demand and Price Forecast

High-priced forecasts are generally more accurate than less-expensive forecasts.

Demand and price forecasts of varying accuracy can be purchased. There are three possible choices:

1. The least accurate set of four quarterly forecasts are automatically generated each quarter on the Summary Sheet. There is no cost for this set of forecasts.
2. An additional, more accurate set of four quarterly forecasts of both demand and price can be obtained for $30,000. When purchased, this forecast will be shown as the second set of forecasts on the Summary Sheet, after the free forecast.
3. The most accurate set of four quarterly forecasts costs $75,000. When this set is purchased, all three forecast sets are provided on the Summary Sheet with the most accurate set coming last.

Accounting Impacts

Performance Report—selling and administrative expenses	$0 or $30,000 or $75,000
Cash Budget—outflows	$0 or $30,000 or $75,000

Manager Objective.   The degree of accuracy of the forecasts is not given; this must be determined by the firm's manager. Continued purchase of more accurate forecasts depends on how much the manager thinks the extra information is worth.

Decision: Purchase of Demand and Price Forecast.   The decision is selected by the appropriate option on the Pro Forma Decision Sheet input form (see Chapter 2).

Product Demanded and Sold

Price and sales demand for units produced are identical for all the firms playing the game for each period of play unless unit price of product or advertising differs among the companies. The actual demand for the past quarter is included on the Summary Sheet (97,383 in Exhibit 4.1 for quarter 1). The per-unit sales price, $100.00 for quarter 1, is given on the sales revenue line of the Performance Report (Exhibit 4.1).

Large opportunity losses result from lost sales.

Rules for Product Demanded and Sold.   There are eight rules:

- Units of product available for sale are always used to meet demand. The units available include beginning inventory plus the units produced during the period.
- All units started in production are finished; there are no raw materials or partially completed units.
- If the unit demand exceeds the amount of goods available, all units are sold and there is a zero ending inventory.
- The unfilled sales demand is lost; it is not added to the company's demand for the following periods. Thus, no back ordering is available in the game.
- The ending inventory is composed of the excess of units available for sale compared to the units demanded.
- *Cash inflows* are obtained on 33 percent of the current quarter's total dollar sales. On sales of $9,738,300 in quarter 1, $3,213,639 resulted in a cash inflow during quarter 1.
- The ending accounts receivable balance contains 67 percent of the current quarter's sales—$6,524,661 in Exhibit 4.2.
- The entire balance in accounts receivable is a *cash inflow* in the following quarter. Thus, $6,524,661 on the quarter 1 statement is collected in quarter 2, together with 33 percent of quarter 2 sales revenue.

Accounting Impacts

Performance Report—sales revenue (97,383 × $100.00)	$9,738,300
Cash Budget—inflows (33% × 97,383 × $100.00)	3,213,639
Position Statement—accounts receivable (67% × 97,383 × $100.00)	6,524,661

Manager Objective.   Profits forgone on sales lost due to inadequate inventory and productive capacity need to be compared to the extra carrying costs of inventory, machine capacity, and plant capacity (including depreciation and the cost of funds invested in these assets). Managers have an optimal investment in productive assets when the profit gained from the expected additional unit sales generated by the additional money invested to produce the extra unit equals the carrying cost of the additional investment. See Chapter 3 for more discussion on strategy formation.

Decision: Unit Production.   The number of units of product to produce is a management decision entered on the Pro Forma Decision Sheet input form (see Chapter 2).

Manager Control of Product Pricing

When price is a management-controlled variable, the unit market demand for the product is variable. The product demand is lower for higher prices, and demand is higher for lower prices. If the unit price decision is not controlled by the manager, an input frame will not be available on the Pro Forma Decision Sheet input form. Instead, an "At market value" message will be provided.

Manager Objective.   The price that maximizes the common shareholders' accumulated wealth is desired. The elasticity of demand to price changes is required before a policy on increasing or decreasing prices can be determined. The requirements for an optimal pricing strategy are covered in Chapter 3 and managerial economics texts.

Decision: Unit Price of Product.   The product price decision is entered as the per-unit price on the Pro Forma Decision Sheet input form (see Chapter 2). If the per-unit price is left blank (value equals zero), the product will automatically be sold at the market price and market demand level that would occur if the price were not controlled. These are the values printed as the actual demand and unit price on the Summary Sheet. If a price is entered, units will be sold at the manager's entered price.

Note: An expected unit price is a required input for pro forma statements. If no unit price is entered, units will be sold at a price of $0 per unit.

Sales Discounts

Managers have an option to select no discount, a 1 percent discount, or a 2 percent discount.

- When no discount is offered, 33 percent of the current quarter's total dollar sales are collected during the sales quarter and 67 percent are collected in the quarter following the sale.
- There are no bad debts and all sales dollars are collected by the quarter after sale.
- The discount policy affects only receivable collections; there are no effects on product sales demand.
- If a discount is offered, more cash is collected from quarterly sales and the investment in accounts receivable is reduced. The collection rate is highest with a 2 percent discount rate.
- The change in receivables for the different discount rates is not provided directly in the game. However, if pro forma statements can be generated in the game, the use of a discount will affect the cash and receivables balances correctly based on the forecasted units demanded and unit price of product.

- With both the 1 and 2 percent discount policies, the receivables that are discounted are all collected in the current period. Two-thirds of all sales that are not discounted are collected in the following period.

The discount policy has no impact on sales demand in the game.

The sales discount is found by subtracting the dollar sales revenue on the Performance Report—$9,738,300 in quarter 1—from the total of units sold times the sales price per unit—$9,738,300 (97,383 × 100.00). In this case, there is no difference in the two numbers in quarter 1 since a zero discount policy was used by the company. The total sales revenue will always be less than the quantity sold times the sales price per unit by the amount of the discount.

Manager Objective.   The next higher discount rate should be adopted if the marginal discount paid to move to this next discount rate divided by the amount of accounts receivable freed from the discount policy is less than the cost of short-term loans.

Decision: Sales Discount on Receivables.   The sales discount policy is selected on the Pro Forma Decision Sheet input form (see Chapter 2).

Cash Management

Short-Term Investments

Short-term investments provide the only other source of company revenue besides product sales.

Short-term investments should be used only for temporary investment of excess funds.

- Excess cash can be invested temporarily until needed in operations or distributed to security holders.
- Managers have control over the risk level of their short-term investments. The safest temporary investment has the lowest expected yield. More risky short-term investments have a higher expected yield. This potential reward is offset by having some outcomes in which investors' return is lower than with a safe or low-risk security. Commonly, negative return outcomes occur with longer-maturity or higher-credit-risk securities.
- The percent quarterly yield on the safest marketable securities held in the just-completed quarter is given on the Summary Sheet as the marketable securities yield. This is 1.362 percent in Exhibit 4.3. The rounding to 1/1000th of 1 percent can cause revenue calculations to diverge slightly from the actual revenue earned.
- The yield on marketable securities in future periods depends mainly on general business conditions and is not forecast in the Summary Sheet.

Example.   In Exhibit 4.2, $200,000 was outstanding at the end of quarter 1. If $500,000 was added for quarter 2, the marketable securities balance would increase to a total of $700,000 and this amount would earn interest for quarter 2. Assuming this to be the case and the quarter 2 interest rate to be 1.350 percent, the following impacts and positions would be on the quarter 2 financial statements.

Accounting Impacts

Performance Report—income from securities	$9,450
Cash Budget—inflows (1.350% × $700,000)	9,450

Cash Budget—outflows—purchase of marketable securities	500,000
Position Statement—marketable securities ($200,000 + $500,000)	700,000

Manager Objective.   The game participant can *form a strategy for estimating the safest marketable security yield* by using other forecast information available on the Summary Sheet. Marketable securities investments are appropriate for the *temporary* investment of surplus funds that will be needed in operations in the next one to two quarters. See Chapter 3 for more details.

Decision: Short-Term Investment.   This decision is entered on the Pro Forma Decision Sheet input form (see Chapter 2). Marketable securities may be purchased and, if they are owned, they may be sold. A minus sign is entered just before the number if a sale is desired. The decision changes the amount of investment in marketable securities. *The balance in marketable securities remains unchanged from the previous quarter if no decision is entered and a forced liquidation of marketable securities does not take place (to be described later).*

Risk Level of Short-Term Investments

- Managers are responsible for determining the risk level they desire. Caution should be exercised in committing large amounts of funds to higher-risk investments until the manager knows the possible downside risk of the decision.
- An increase in risk of short-term investments is achieved in the game by selecting a risk level from 0 (zero) for no risk through 9 for the highest risk level.
- A 0 (zero) is used to invest in the safest marketable securities, the equivalent of 90-day Treasury bills. No default or interest rate risk exists with the safest possible short-term investment. The investor will earn the economy-wide, equilibrium, 90-day (one quarter), short-term interest rate.
- The highest-risk investment (having an entry of 9) is a perpetual security that can either lose up to 40 percent of its ending period value from an increase in credit risk or gain up to 45 percent of its value from a decrease in credit risk in one quarter.
- All short-term investments outstanding (not just new additions to short-term investments) have the risk category selected.

Decision: Risk of Short-Term Investment.   Risk of short-term investment (0 to 9) is entered on the Pro Forma Decision Sheet input form (see Chapter 2). The risk (0 to 9) can be changed each quarter.

Cash Shortages and Marketable Securities Liquidation

In the case of a cash shortage at the end of a period, the marketable securities are automatically retired with a penalty charge of 3 percent of the cash shortage. If c is the cash shortage, the marketable securities retired, S_m, would be:

$$S_m = 1.03c$$

The penalty is imposed to encourage careful, accurate cash management.

Example.   Assume a company has a cash shortage of $200,000 at the end of quarter 2 and a quarter 1 marketable securities balance of $1,000,000. The marketable securities balance would automatically be reduced to $794,000 (or $1,000,000 – [$200,000 × 1.03]). The marketable securities balance on the quarter 2 Position Statement would be $794,000, and the account penalty loan interest on the Performance Report would be $6,000 (or 3% × $200,000). Note that the company still earned the quarterly marketable security yield (1.35%) on the $200,000 in liquidated securities since they were liquidated at the end of the quarter. An additional tax reduction of $2,400 (0.4 × $6,000) with a tax rate of 40 percent results from the decision, leading to a final cash balance of $2,400, even though there was an initial cash shortage.

The inclusion of the 3 percent liquidation fee under the penalty loan interest account is a nonstandard accounting treatment. It is used in the game so that the manager can easily check for liquidity shortages during the quarter by examining for a balance in the penalty loan interest account in the income statement.

Warning. Since final positive cash balances exist even though an FG company has cash shortages, forced liquidated marketable securities, and penalty loans, managers would be in error to look at their cash balance to detect cash shortages and cash stock-outs. The Penalty-Loan Interest line on the Quarterly Performance Report (Exhibit 4.1) needs to be checked to see if a cash shortage occurred. The extent of the cash stock-out is then found by determining the forced reduction in the Marketable Securities account and the size of the Short-Term Penalty Loan, both shown on the Position Statement (Exhibit 4.2).

> *When cash is short, the game automatically liquidates marketable securities with a penalty.*

Accounting Impacts

Performance Report—income from securities	$ 13,500
Cash Budget—inflows (1.35% × $1,000,000)	13,500
Cash Budget—outflow (3% × $200,000)	6,000
Performance Report—penalty loan interest	6,000
Cash Budget—inflow ($200,000 × 1.03)	206,000
Position Statement—marketable securities ($1,000,000 – $206,000)	794,000
Performance Report—Taxes decrease by (0.4 × 6,000)	2,400
Position Statement—Cash balance increases from 0 to 2,400	

Manager Objective.   The long-term objective is to minimize the combination of carrying costs for maintaining cash balances and stock-out costs from having insufficient cash balances. This is achieved by setting cash balances so that the expected per period carrying cost for the last dollar added to the safety-stock of cash is equal to the expected per period stock-out cost from this same last dollar being added to cash. See Chapter 3 for further discussion.

Decision.   The decision is automatically performed by FG.

Cash Shortages and Short-Term Penalty Loans

> *Penalty loans are automatically issued for end-of-quarter cash shortages.*

- If the marketable securities balance is insufficient to cover the cash shortage, a penalty loan equal to the remaining cash shortage is automatically advanced.
- An 8 percent quarterly rate of interest is charged on the loan.
- The penalty debt is automatically retired in the following period with no additional interest charged.

An example will indicate how penalty loan balance, taxes, and new cash balance are determined.

Example.   Assume there is a cash deficit of $210,000, a marketable securities balance of $103,000 that earned 1.35% or $1,390.50, and a 40 percent tax rate. First, the decrease in the deficit, c, resulting from the liquidation of securities, S_m, at a discount rate of 3 percent is calculated. Solving for c, $100,000 of the deficit is eliminated:

$$1.03c = S_m$$

$$1.03c = \$103,000$$

$$c = \$100,000$$

This leaves a $110,000 deficit and a $3,000 interest charge for liquidating securities. The penalty loan balance must cover both the revised shortage, $110,000, and the current-period penalty-loan interest. Combining terms, calculate the loan, L, to be equal to the cash shortage plus 8% times the cash shortage not covered with securities.

$$L = \$110,000 + [\$110,000 \times 0.08]$$

$$L = \$118,800.$$

This temporarily leaves the firm with a cash balance of zero. The additional interest charge, $11,800 (or $3,000 + [$110,000 × 0.08]), is an additional current-period tax deductible expense. All other-quarter cash transactions (including the cash flow from taxes on income) are recorded before the penalty balance is determined. Therefore, there is an additional $11,800 of deductible expense. This reduces the tax and current-period cash payment for taxes that had already been paid by $4,720 (or 40% × $11,800). This $4,720 is the new and final cash balance.

Accounting Impacts

Performance Report—income from securities	$ 1,390
Cash Budget—inflows (1.35% × $103,000)	1,390
Cash Budget—outflow (3% × $100,000 + 8% × $110,000) × (1 − .40)	7,080
Performance Report—penalty-loan interest	11,800
Performance Report—income tax (.40 × $11,800) reduction in tax of	−4,720
Cash Budget—inflow ($100,000 + 110,000)	210,000
Position Statement—marketable securities ($103,000 − $103,000)	0
Position Statement—short-term penalty loan ($110,000 × 1.08)	118,800
Position Statement—final cash balance	4,720

Manager Objective.   The long-term objective is to minimize the combination of carrying costs coming from maintaining expected cash balances when a positive cash balance is generated and facing expected stock-out costs when cash shortages occur. This is achieved by setting cash balances so that the expected per period carrying cost for the last dollar added to the safety-stock of cash is equal to the expected per period stock-out cost from this same last dollar being added to cash. See Chapter 3 for further discussion.

Decision.   The decision is automatically performed by FG.

Production Costs

The manufacturing cost components of the firm are materials, direct labor, warehouse fees, plant, machinery, capital budgeting projects, other overhead, and both plant and equipment depreciation.

Materials

The company's product is fabricated from raw materials. The following conditions apply to the input materials required to make a unit of final product:

- One unit of material is required to produce one unit of finished product.
- The cost per unit of material is $15.00, unless changed by the instructor or in case of inflation. The cost of a unit of material is given on the Summary Sheet each quarter. (See Exhibit 4.3.)
- The quantity required for actual unit production is automatically purchased within the game. Thus, a specific decision on materials is not required.
- There are no material or work-in-progress inventories at the end of a period.
- The period's material cost is a current-period cost of goods produced and appears in the Performance Report within the cost of goods sold section.
- A cash *outflow* for 90 percent of the quarterly material cost occurs in the current period. The remaining 10 percent is part of the accounts payable balance (Exhibit 4.2) and is a cash outflow in the following quarter.

For example, assume 100,000 units will be produced in quarter 2.

Accounting Impacts

Performance Report—materials (100,000 × $15.00)	$1,500,000
Cash Budget—outflows	1,350,000
Position Statement—accounts payable	150,000

Decision.   The decision is automatically performed by FG.

Direct Labor

Direct labor costs are incurred in producing the product.

- The direct labor cost required to produce one unit varies for different unit volume production levels. Exhibit 4.5 is taken from the Summary Sheet (Exhibit 4.3). The exhibit indicates the four different possible initial per-unit labor costs for quarter 2.
- The per-unit labor costs for different levels of production can change over time depending on the capital budgeting projects adopted and expired and the level of inflation. The impact from the "Capital Budgeting Projects" section is described later in this chapter.
- The labor costs required to complete the actual units produced in quarter 1 of $3,500,000 (or [60,000 × $39.00] + [40,000 × $29.00]) are automatically recorded in the game. No decision is required by the manager to secure or pay the labor costs.

Required materials, labor, and warehouse costs are automatically purchased and paid within the game.

EXHIBIT 4.5   Direct Labor Costs

	Units			
	First 60,000	*Next 40,000*	*Next 20,000*	*Over 120,000*
Labor cost	$39.00	$29.00	$25.00	$33.00

- The quarter's total direct labor costs are presented on the Performance Report in the cost of goods sold section.
- A *cash outflow* equal to 90 percent of the direct labor costs occurs in the current quarter; the other 10 percent becomes part of the accounts payable balance (Exhibit 4.2). The accounts payable balance is paid in the next quarter.

Accounting Impacts

Performance Report—direct labor (60,000 × $39.00 + 40,000 × $29.00)	$3,500,000
Cash Budget—outflows	3,150,000
Position Statement—accounts payable	350,000

Decision.   The decision is automatically performed by FG.

Warehouse Fees

- Warehouse fees are charged on ending inventories on a per-unit basis.
- There are three different per-unit charges: $1.00 on the first 2,000 units, $3.00 on the next 5,000 units, and $8.00 per unit thereafter.
- The Performance Report's stated warehouse fees of $60,408 are derived from the ending inventory balance of 12,426 units and the warehouse fee schedule—[2,000 × $1.00] + [5,000 × $3.00] + [5,426 × $8.00] = $60,408.
- The warehouse fee schedule remains the same throughout the game.
- Warehouse fees are a current quarterly *cash outflow*.

Accounting Impacts

Performance Report—warehousing costs (see above)	$60,408
Cash Budget—outflows	60,408

Decision.   The decision is automatically performed by FG.

Plant

The fixed plant order cost of $250,000 is often overlooked when preparing the cash budget by hand.

Plant capacity is required, in addition to machine capacity, to produce the product. New plant capacity has to be purchased as product demand increases and/or old plant expires.

- Actual unit production in a given quarter cannot exceed the operating plant capacity for that quarter.
- Plant capacity levels for the next four quarters are given on the Summary Sheet each quarter in the section "Information for Future Quarters." The plant capacity and depreciation charges, which are not given on the Summary Sheet for the remaining periods beyond quarter 5, are provided in Exhibit 4.6.
- The plant capacity information on the Summary Sheet is automatically adjusted for expirations or new additions.
- **It takes two quarters to build a new plant.** For example, a plant ordered in quarter 2 is not usable until quarter 4.
- A plant has a life of 20 quarters. For each unit of plant, one unit of product can be produced in each of its 20 periods, starting with the quarter when the capacity comes on line. This would be in quarter 4 in the example just provided.

- The plant capacity expires whether or not it is used.
- There is no end-of-life salvage value or removal cost for expired plant.
- Plant per-unit purchase price is listed in the Summary Sheet ($321 for quarter 2). The general level of business activity and inflation affect the unit price of plant capacity.
- There is also a fixed $250,000 order cost every time plant capacity is purchased.
- The total plant cost is a *cash outflow* in the period it is ordered.
- Plant is depreciated on a straight-line basis. One-twentieth of the original cost is depreciated each quarter. Depreciation starts two quarters after purchase, when the added plant capacity becomes operational.
- The current plant depreciation is included in the cost of goods sold section of the Performance Report. The depreciation on the plant in each of the next four quarters, assuming that there are no new plant additions, is included in the Summary Sheet.
- The original cost of all past plants purchased less accumulated depreciation is presented in the fixed assets section of the Position Statement every quarter.

Accounting Impacts.   Plant purchases of 20,000 units at $321 per unit:

Position Statement—plant	$6,670,000
Cash Budget—outflows (20,000 × $321 + $250,000)	6,670,000

Accounting Impacts.   Depreciation for quarter 2:

Performance Report—depreciation: plant (from Exhibit 4.3)	$1,300,000
Position Statement—plant (quarter 1 balance of $7,165,250 – $1,300,000)	5,865,250

Note: In the above example with a purchase of 20,000 units of plant, the quarter 2 Position Statement—plant account would be $12,535,250 ($5,865,250 + $6,670,000).

Managers often overlook the two-period delay that occurs when purchasing plant capacity.

Decision: Units of Plant Capacity Purchased.   Units of plant capacity purchased for a quarter are entered on the Pro Forma Decision Sheet input form (see Chapter 2). The number of units ordered is automatically reset to zero on the next actual decision form.

Machinery

Machinery is needed to produce units. The following conditions apply to machinery:

- A unit of machine capacity can produce one unit.
- The actual units produced in a given quarter cannot exceed the company's operating machine capacity for that quarter.

EXHIBIT **4.6**   **Plant Capacity and Depreciation beyond Quarter 5**

	Period					
	6	7	8	9	10	After 10
Capacity	50,000	50,000	25,000	25,000	25,000	0
Depreciation	$667,500	$667,500	$313,750	$313,750	$313,750	0

EXHIBIT 4.7 **Machinery Capacity and Depreciation beyond Quarter 5**

	Period			
	6	7	8	After 8
Capacity	60,000	5,000	5,000	0
Depreciation	$311,250	$22,500	$22,500	0

- Information on the machine capacity and depreciation for each of the next four quarters is provided on the Summary Sheet each quarter. The depreciation and capacity levels of machinery in future quarters beyond 5 are listed in Exhibit 4.7.
- Machinery capacity and depreciation information on the Summary Sheet is automatically adjusted for expirations and new additions.
- A unit of machine capacity purchased in one period becomes operational in the next period. For example, machine capacity added in quarter 2 is not available for producing units until quarter 3.

Production is limited to the lesser of plant or machine capacity.

- Machinery is depreciated on a straight-line basis. The depreciation rate is equal to one-eighth of the original cost each period. Depreciation starts in the quarter after acquisition, when the machinery becomes operational. The machine depreciation for the current period is included with the depreciation of capital budgeting projects on the Performance Report.

- The purchase of machinery results in a *cash outflow* in the quarter of purchase. *The cost of a single unit of capacity for the coming quarter is given on the Summary Sheet.* The machinery cost varies from quarter to quarter and is related to the general level of business activity and inflation the firm will face.

- Excess machinery can be stored at no additional cost. Therefore, the unit machine capacity can exceed the unit plant capacity. Production is limited to the lesser of plant or machine capacity.
- Machinery has an eight-quarter useful life.[1] At the end of its last period, it is removed with no additional costs or cash flows.
- Machinery expires whether or not it is used. Nonuse, including storage, does not postpone the expiration of machine potential.
- Machine capacity can only be purchased. Sale, abandonment, and removal are not available options in the game.

The one-period delay in use of added machine capacity must be considered.

- The machinery and equipment account of the Position Statement includes the original cost of both machinery and capital budgeting projects less accumulated depreciation.

Accounting Impacts. Machine purchases total 15,000 units at $47 per unit.

Cash Budget—outflows (15,000 × $47)	$705,000
Position Statement—machinery and equipment	705,000

---

[1]A special option violates this condition. See the extraordinary item, "fire eliminates inventory and machine capacity."

Accounting Impacts.   Depreciation for quarter 2 totals

Performance Report—depreciation: mach. and equip. (from Exhibit 4.3)	$478,125
Position Statement—mach. and equip. (quarter 1 of $2,008,125 – $478,125)	1,530,000

Manager Objective.   Profits forgone on sales lost due to inadequate inventory and productive capacity need to be compared to the extra carrying costs of inventory, machine capacity, and plant capacity (including depreciation and the cost of funds invested in these assets). Managers have an optimal investment in productive assets when the profit gained from the expected additional unit sales generated by the additional funds invested to produce the extra unit equals the carrying cost of the additional investment. See Chapter 3 for more on strategy formation.

Decision: Units of Machine Capacity Purchased.   Units of machinery purchased for a quarter are entered on the Pro Forma Decision Sheet input form (see Chapter 2). The number of units ordered is automatically reset to zero on the next actual decision form.

Capital Budgeting Projects

The following rules apply to the capital budgeting projects:

- Two new possible capital budgeting projects are available for purchase *each quarter*. The manager has the option of accepting both projects, rejecting both projects, or selecting either A or B while rejecting the other.
- A new A and B are offered each period and the above selection options are again available. For example, the acceptance of A in quarter 2 does not limit the further acceptance of another A in any future quarter.
- The basic information on each quarter's two projects, A and B, is presented in the capital budgeting projects for next quarter section of the Summary Sheet (Exhibit 4.8). Exhibit 4.8 contains this information for quarter 2 projects.
- Project A always has an 8-quarter life and a capacity of 100,000 units, while B has a 12-quarter life and a capacity of 120,000 units.
- The project cost is a current-period *cash outflow* at the date of purchase. Project A would cost $659,280 in Exhibit 4.8.
- A project affects changes in the other overhead account for each quarter of its life. Project A above reduces other overhead charges by $15,340 in each quarter 2 through 9.
- Projects also affect changes in the per-unit labor costs covered in the "Direct Labor" section of this chapter. When adopted, the projects reduce labor costs in their first quarter of use by the amount listed under the

EXHIBIT 4.8   Capital Budgeting Alternatives for Next Quarter

	Life	Cost	Unit Capacity	Overhead Saving	Unit Labor Sav. Qtr. 2	Change/Qtr. Labor Sav.
A	2 yrs.	$659,280	100,000	$15,340	$0.82	$0.03
B	3 yrs.	$513,342	120,000	–$8,102	$0.85	–$0.01

heading "Unit labor sav., Qt. *x*," an abbreviation for "Unit labor savings in quarter *x*." Referring to Exhibit 4.8, this is 82 cents per-unit for project A.
- This per-unit savings applies for up to 100,000 units produced for project A and up to 120,000 for project B.
- The capital budgeting projects become operational immediately and generate savings and cost changes in the period purchased. Therefore, the projected per-unit labor costs and total dollar overhead costs on the current-period Summary Sheet need to be changed to reflect the impact of the new project(s) acquired.

Example.   When A is accepted, the other overhead charge for period 2 would have to be revised downward by $15,340, to $184,660. The labor costs for period 2 would become $38.18 (or $39.00 – $0.82) for the first 60,000 units and $28.18 (or $29.00 – $0.82) for the next 40,000 units. These changes would have to be used if pro forma statements are being prepared by hand. Corrections will automatically be incorporated into pro forma statements generated on the computer.

- The quarterly per-unit labor savings of a project can change throughout the life of the project. The amount of this change is presented in the Summary Sheet under the title "Change/Qtr. Labor Sav.," an abbreviation of "the change per quarter in per-unit labor savings." With the example in Exhibit 4.8, the quarterly change in labor savings for A is 0.03. For example, the labor savings per unit for A and B over the life of the two projects are given in Exhibit 4.9.
- The Summary Sheet in future quarters will automatically include the effects of the accepted capital budgeting project on both the other overhead and the labor cost sections of the Summary Sheet over the life of the accepted projects.

Example.   If project A were accepted, the quarter 2 output statements would list quarter 3 labor costs as $38.15 (or $39.00 – .85) for the first 60,000 units, and $28.15 (or $29.00 – .85) for the next 40,000 units. Since A's capacity is only 100,000 units, the labor cost rates on the next 20,000 units and those over 120,000 would remain unchanged at $25.00 and $33.00, respectively.

- The capital budgeting projects are production line improvements that reduce labor costs, power consumption, and other overhead items. **They do not increase or affect in any manner the machine or plant capacity required to produce units.**
- The capacity potential of the capital budgeting projects remains at 100,000 for A and 120,000 for B even if plant or machine capacity falls below this level. For example, assume that in quarters 2 through 5 the machine capacity is 80,000 units and A is purchased in quarter 2. In quarter 6 and

EXHIBIT 4.9   **Quarter 2 Projects' per-unit Labor Cost Savings**

						Period						
		2	3	4	5	6	7	8	9	10	11	12	13
Savings (cents)	A	82	85	88	91	94	97	100	103	—	—	—	—
	B	85	84	83	82	81	80	79	78	77	76	75	74

on, machine capacity increases to 100,000 units and savings in labor costs can now be generated on 100,000 units for A and the first 100,000 of the then existing project B's capacity of 120,000.

- Depreciation is straight-line, equal to 1/8th of A's or 1/12th of B's initial project cost each quarter.

- Depreciation on capital budgeting projects is included with depreciation on machinery in the Performance Report. Depreciation charges for each of the next four quarters on all past accepted capital budgeting projects is included on the Summary Sheet in the section "Depreciation: Projects."

- The original cost less accumulated depreciation of the capital budgeting projects is included with the net machinery in the machinery and equipment account of the Position Statement.

Accounting Impacts.   Project A is acquired in quarter 2.

Cash Budget—outflows	$659,280
Position Statement—machinery and equipment ($659,280 – $82,410)	576,870
Performance Report—depreciation: mach. and equip. ($659,280 /8)	82,410

Additional marginal effects assuming production in quarter 2 of 100,000 include:

Cash Budget—inflows (reduction in outflows)	$97,000
Performance Report—direct labor (reduction)	82,000
Performance Report—other overhead costs (reduction)	15,000

Manager Objective.   Net present value analysis or the internal rate of return procedure should be used to evaluate projects. The cost of capital needs to be derived quarterly and used as the discount or hurdle rate for the projects. Positive net present value projects or projects with an internal rate of return greater than the cost of capital should be accepted. If the projects are acceptable, external funds should be sought, if necessary, to finance the projects.

Decisions: Capital Budgeting Projects A and B.   Capital budgeting projects are acquired by selecting the "Yes" option for a project on the Pro Forma Decision Sheet input form (see Chapter 2). The items are left blank if no purchase is desired.

Other Overhead

The other overhead costs account includes fixed production expenses except depreciation.

This includes items like fixed lease and rent commitments, property taxes and assessments, the minimum fixed utility costs, and minimum indirect labor costs for plant maintenance.

- The current period's other overhead costs are included in the Performance Report in the cost of goods sold section. The other overhead costs for the next four quarters are included in the Summary Sheet.

- Adjustments to the other overhead costs account through the acquisition and expiration of capital budgeting projects were covered earlier. Except for these adjustments, the other overhead costs remain at a constant $200,000 throughout the game.

- Ninety percent of the period's other overhead charges are a *cash outflow* in the period they occur. Ten percent are deferred and become part of the accounts payable on the position statement together with 10 percent of both the total materials and labor costs. The adjustments are automatic and not manager-controlled.

- If the plant and machine unit operating capacities are both at zero units, the production segment of the firm is considered liquidated and the other overhead charges are zero.

Accounting Impacts.   Projects A and B are not acquired in quarter 2.

Cash Budget—outflows	$180,000
Position Statement—accounts payable	20,000
Performance Report—other overhead costs	200,000

Decision.   The decision is automatically performed by FG.

Summary on Production Costs

The Performance Report includes all the quarterly cost effects covered in this subsection. The sum of the period materials, direct labor, warehousing fees, depreciation, and other overhead costs is the total production costs.

The *average unit production cost*—$70.39 in quarter 1—is found by dividing the actual unit production (100,000) into the total production costs ($7,038,533). This information is provided on the Performance Report on the production costs line.

Note: The per-unit cost of $70.39 contains rounding error since the cost is actually $70.38533 per unit. The per-unit costs or prices throughout the set of financial statements times the number of units will often not equal the actual account balance. Goods available for sale include the beginning inventory and period production costs. *Average costing* is used in the game. An average cost of a unit sold is the sum of the beginning inventory balance ($733,567) and production costs ($7,038,533) divided by the sum of beginning inventory units (9,809) and units produced (100,000). As Exhibit 4.1 shows, this is $70.78 (or $7,772,100/109,809) per unit. *Ending inventory* is also valued on the average cost basis—$879,492 for quarter 1.

Selling and Administrative Expenses

Selling and administrative expenses include executive salaries, central office administrative costs, advertising expense, the costs of additional price and demand forecasts, and costs of sales and distribution systems.

The following conditions apply to the selling and administrative expenses account:

- There is a fixed cost component of $1,000,000 each quarter.
- This fixed cost component is not charged in any period when operating plant capacity is zero units.
- There is a variable cost component equal to 5 percent of the quarterly sales revenue listed on the Performance Report.
- Advertising (described next) is a current-period expense included in selling and administrative expenses.
- Costs of additional price and demand forecasts of $30,000 or $75,000 are part of selling and administrative expenses.

- The selling and administrative expenses quarterly charge is a *cash outflow* in the period it occurs. Thus, from Exhibit 4.1, the account balance, $1,486,915, calculated for quarter 1 was paid in cash in quarter 1.
- The selling and administrative expenses are automatically calculated within the simulation and charged to expense and credited to cash each quarter.

Accounting Impacts.   Additional forecasts and advertising are not used in quarter 2.

Cash Budget—outflows ($1,000,000 + [.05 × $9,738,300])	$1,486,915
Performance Report—selling and administrative expenses	1,486,915

Manager Objective.   The fixed quarterly and variable administrative and selling costs are operating costs that must be covered before a company achieves profitability and sufficient return to cover the cost of capital. If this objective is not expected to be achieved in the long run, the company should be closed or liquidated. Objectives with forecast costs and advertising are in their respective subsections.

Decision.   The decision is automatically performed by FG.

Advertising Costs

Advertising costs can be incurred to increase product demand. The relative shift in demand caused by advertising is impacted by both the general economic level of activity and the company's adopted pricing policy.

Advertising is reported as part of the selling and administrative expenses on the Performance Report; it is a *cash outflow* in the quarter of entry.

Manager Objective.   The manager needs to determine an optimal advertising expense that should be paid each quarter. Advertising should be added if the marginal dollar of expense returns at least the dollar cost plus the cost of capital at the end of the quarter. See the discussion of advertising in Chapter 3.

Decision: Advertising.   The total dollar amount of quarterly advertising costs is entered on the Pro Forma Decision Sheet input form (see Chapter 2). The impact of advertising in a given quarter is not dependent on prior levels of advertising.

Extraordinary Items

Unexpected one-shot events that require additional management planning and often a revision in the company strategy can be initiated by the instructor. The labor strike, extraordinary loss or gain, and fire options that follow can occur at any time at the instructor's discretion.

Labor Strike

- The labor strike is a special option initiated by the instructor.
- Managers first receive a statement about an impending strike. The announcement appears after the Summary Sheet on the firm's output. It states, "Bargaining with the labor union is continuing and in the next period the firm

must either meet the union's demands or face a possible one-period strike." For example, if this were quarter 10, the strike could take place in quarter 12. The instructor also can initiate a wildcat strike without any warning given.

- The strike possibility occurs for all firms playing the game.

Three options are available to the manager:

1. All union demands can be refused, with an instructor set percent chance for a strike lasting only one quarter. If the strike occurs, production is halted for one quarter.
2. With a $6.00 increase in labor cost per unit, the probability of a one-period strike would be one-half of the instructor's probability of having a strike.
3. The strike can be averted with a $15.00 increase in labor cost per unit. Labor cost increases are initiated for all levels of production starting with the period of the possible strike. The settlement choice can allow some firms to produce, while others are idle for the period. The instructor has the ability to have more than one possible strike during the game.

Manager Objective.   The manager should examine the trade-off between losses from missed production versus increased labor costs throughout the game. The production and inventory levels before the strike might also require changes depending on the modified production costs and strategy of the firm.

Decision: Labor Strike.   The *strike settlement decision* is selected with a decision option available on the Pro Forma Decision Sheet input form (see Chapter 2) when an impending possible strike is coming. The option is shown on the screen only if there is a forthcoming strike possibility that is not a wildcat strike.

Extraordinary Loss or Gain

- An instructor-initiated option causes a large cash outflow or inflow and an extraordinary loss or gain.
- There is no warning of an impending problem unless the instructor wishes to provide the information in advance.
- In the period of occurrence, the Performance Report account titled "extraordinary items" will indicate the dollar amount of the extraordinary item.

Manager Objective.   The manager must assess the new position of the firm after this event and adjust the future policies to reflect the current performance and position of the company.

Decision.   No active decision is made by the manager.

Fire

A fire can eliminate inventory and machine capacity.

- Initiated by the instructor, this option eliminates all ending inventories and an instructor-specified percentage of machine capacity.

- No warning is given that the fire will occur; the statement "YOUR FIRM HAS HAD A FIRE" is provided if one occurs.
- Unlike the real world, the fires are systematic, occurring to all firms in the game at the same time. The option is applied to a firm at the end of the quarter after all the period's production and sales have taken place.
- Inventory is insured and cash is received for the dollar cost of the ending inventory balance.
- No cash is received for lost machine capacity. The event is extraordinary in nature and the lost machine value is charged to the extraordinary items account.
- The machine capacity in all future periods is cut by a specific percentage. The machine capacity figures on the previous and current Summary Sheets can be compared to determine the percentage of capacity lost.

Manager Objective.   This option requires extra management planning with both acquisition of funds and a reformulating of a production strategy. The lost production capacity that will exist until the lost machine capacity is replaced will also negatively affect short-run future performance. Managers need to consider possible adjustments in the capital structure due to this increased company risk. The cost of capital will have to be monitored to determine changes that affect all future company investment decisions.

Decision.   No active decision is made by the manager.

Loans and Debt Costs

Both company performance and level of financial leverage affect interest rates.

Debt costs or expenses arise from the use of short-term loans, the two intermediate-term loans, bonds, and the penalty loan. In the game, the interest rate charged on debt, excluding the penalty loan (described earlier), is determined by five items:

1. An *underlying yield curve* provides the relationship between interest rates for debt with different maturities. The yield curve in the game can have a constant, positive, or negative slope. Examination of the yields on debt of different maturities can help in isolating the company's yield curve. Instructors can change the slope of the yield curve during the game.
2. *Economic conditions* affect the yields on debt. In an expanding economy, demand for funds is high and the interest rate structure on all debt and securities is higher. The reverse holds with an expected downturn.
3. *Inflation* increases the interest rates for all types of debt issues other than the penalty loan with a greater impact on longer maturity debt.
4. *Risk of insolvency* is related to the firm's long-run ability to meet debt payments. This, in turn, is a function of the profitability, variability in profitability, and debt-equity structure of the firm. As the likelihood of insolvency increases, all debt costs increase, and the longer-term obligations become relatively more expensive than the shorter-term obligations.
5. A *temporary size of offering premium* adjusts for intra-period debt changes. The premium serves as a constraint against massive single-period debt offerings. The premium represents a concession needed to

increase demand for the debt sufficiently to sell all the debt offered to the market for companies with greater amounts of financial leverage. In the game, **cost increases of 0.125 percent per million dollars** of quarterly debt offered in a given quarter are imposed.

Example.   The rate for bonds for quarter 2 from Exhibit 4.3 is 1.754 percent. Assume that a total $6.5 million of two-year debt, three-year debt, and bonds are to be issued. The specific offering of bonds would have a required yield of 2.504 percent (or 1.754% + [0.125% × 6]). Likewise, the two-year debt would have a yield of 2.665 percent, and three-year loans' yield would be 2.604 percent since the 0.75 percent premium (0.125% × 6) would be added to the Exhibit 4.3 rates.

Manager Objective.   Managers must estimate the percent cost of any new financing using step 5 above and "Rates on funding in quarter x" of the Summary Sheet in deriving estimates of the actual quarterly rates on debt. These estimates are required as input information in generating pro forma statements both in FG and by hand.

Short-Term Loans

Temporary funds can be obtained through short-term loans. The following rules apply:

- An immediate *cash inflow* equals the size of the issued short-term loan.
- A short-term loan is issued for four quarters and is repaid in equal installments.
- A *cash outflow* is equal to
  a. Twenty-five percent of the current quarter's short-term loan just issued, plus
  b. The installments due on the previous quarters' short-term loans, presented on the Summary Sheet, plus
  c. The interest on all outstanding short-term loan balances for the quarter.
- Retirement is automatic.
- Retirement before maturity is not possible.
- The interest rate is included in the "Rates on funding in quarter x" section of the Summary Sheet. This new rate must be adjusted upward for the size of new issues premium just covered. The adjusted rate is applied to all short-term loans.

Example.   The rate for the company for quarter 2 is 1.981 percent from Exhibit 4.3. If no new short-term loans are issued, the 1.981 percent rate applies to all outstanding short-term loans for quarter 2. If new short-term loans are issued in quarter 2, the manager will have to estimate the effect of the new issue on the rate. Assume the prior example with a premium of 0.75 percent. The revised rate of 2.731 percent (1.981% + 0.750%) would be applied to the entire outstanding short-term loan's balance.

Accounting Impacts.   The company issues $800,000 of short-term debt and no other debt.

Cash Budget—inflow (issuance)	$800,000
Cash Budget—outflow (first repayment installment + interest)	215,848
Position Statement—short-term loans payable	600,000
Performance Report—short-term bank interest (1.981% × $800,000)	15,848

Decision: Short-Term Loans.   The short-term loans issuance decision is on the decision form (see Chapter 2). All financing decisions are automatically reset to zero for each new set of quarterly decisions. The status quo is to have no financing; an active decision is required by managers to issue any new financing by entering the amount desired each quarter.

Short-Term Penalty Loans

See the "Cash Shortages and Short-Term Penalty Loans" subsection in the "Cash Management" section.

Intermediate-Term Loans

Two- or three-year intermediate-term loans can be issued. Here are the rules that apply to intermediate-term loans:

- Intermediate-term loans are issued for 8 or 12 quarters and are repaid in equal installments.
- The loan is taken out at the beginning of the quarter with a resultant *cash inflow* equal to the total loan issued.
- Repayment of the first installment starts at the end of the quarter of issue.
- Retirement is automatic.
- The cost rates on the new intermediate loans, before the size of offering risk premium, are given on the Summary Sheet in the section on "Rates on funding in quarter *x*."
- The outstanding debt yields given on the Summary Sheet are weighted average costs of all debt issued of a given class, either the two- or three-year loan or bonds.
- A standard accounting procedure is used in reporting debt balances. Debt retired within one year (four quarters) is listed as current liabilities on the Position Statement (Exhibit 4.2). All debt maturing after four quarters is listed in the long-term liabilities section.
- The repayment in each of the next four quarters for each class of debt is given in the Summary Sheet under principal repayment on debt.
- The size of all the installments for the two-year loan installments in quarters beyond those shown on the Summary Sheet is $312,500 in each of quarters 6 through 8.
- Retirement before maturity is allowed without penalty or extra cost. The most recent quarterly installments are retired first. The outstanding debt yields from the Summary Sheet are unaffected by retirement. A loan with a weighted average yield derived from combining all of the prior issues' balances still outstanding is retired. A specific previous issue cannot be retired. The currently due quarterly installment is paid at the end of the quarter and cannot be retired in advance.
- The interest payable in the coming quarter is presented on the Summary Sheet each period. Additional interest from new issues would be calculated using the size of offering premium and the appropriate (two- or three-year) rate for the coming period, listed on the summary sheet under "Rates on funding in quarter *x*."

- The decrease in interest coming from a retirement is calculated by applying the appropriate debt rate from the yields of outstanding debt section of the Summary Sheet to the amount being retired. For interest calculation purposes, a retirement is viewed as taking place at the beginning of the quarter.
- A *cash outflow* occurs each quarter. It is composed of
  - a. The interest on the intermediate-term debt, plus
  - b. The principal repayment on intermediate-term debt listed on the Summary Sheet, plus
  - c. The first quarterly installment on any new intermediate debt offered in the current quarter, plus
  - d. The dollar amount of prepayment of intermediate-term debt.

Accounting Impacts.　The company issues $2,400,000 of three-year debt for quarter 2 and no other debt. The impact of already outstanding intermediate-term debt is also included.

Cash Budget—inflow (issuance)		$2,400,000
Cash Budget—outflows:		
Prior 2-year loan installment		312,500
New 3-year loan installment		200,000
Prior 3-year loan installment		300,000
Intermediate interest (on prior debt from Exhibit 4.3)		83,031
Interest on new 3-year loan ([1.854% + 2 × 0.125%] × $2,400,000)		50,496
Performance Report—intermediate-term loan interest		
($83,031 + $50,496)		133,527
Position Statement—intermediate-term debt maturing:		
2-year debt ($312,500 × 4)	$1,250,000	
Prior 3-year loan ($300,000 [qtr. 3 installment])	300,000	
New 3-year loan (4 × $200,000)	$ 800,000	2,350,000
Position Statement—long-term liabilities		
2-year loans (2 × $312,500 [qtrs. 7 and 8])	$ 625,000	
3-year loans (7 × $200,000 [qtrs. 7–13])	1,400,000	2,025,000

Warning: Participants often have difficulty in determining the outstanding balance of a given type of debt and in projecting the consequence on the Position Statement of a newly issued debt. This arises from the standard accounting convention of showing the debt coming due in one year (four quarters hence) in the current portion of the liabilities while including the remainder in a long-term liability account. Managers in the game often erroneously disregard or overlook the current liability component. This leads to errors if a pro forma is being estimated by hand and when debt balances are used in making company decisions, like determining the company's weighted average cost of capital.

Decision: Intermediate-Term Debt.　The decision is entered on the Pro Forma Decision Sheet input form (see Chapter 2). A given type of loan can be either issued or retired in each period. *A minus sign immediately in front of the number indicates a retirement decision.* All financing decisions are automatically reset to zero for each new set of quarterly decisions. The "status quo" is to have no financing; an active decision is required by managers to issue any new financing by entering the amount of additional financing to issue or retire each quarter.

Long-Term Bonds

Bonds have the longest maturity of the available debt instruments and are often used as a source of permanent funds in obtaining financial leverage. The following rules apply:

The $50,000 flotation cost of a new issue is often overlooked. Errors in available funds and interest expense result.

- Long-term bonds are issued for 10 years (40 quarters). A bond issued at the beginning of the quarter generates a current quarterly cash inflow.
- Bonds are repayable in 40 equal quarterly principal installments starting at the end of the issuance quarter. Retirement is automatic. A decision input is not required by the manager.
- Yield on a new long-term bond to be issued, before adjustment for the size of offering risk premium, is indicated on the Summary Sheet in the section on "Rates on funding in quarter x."
- The yield on outstanding bonds, given on the Summary Sheet, is a weighted cost of all debt issued. Interest due in the coming period on the current outstanding bonds is presented on the Summary Sheet. The interest charges for the previous period are on the Performance Report in the financial expenses section.
- There is a fixed $50,000 flotation cost every time new bonds are issued that is a current-period *cash outflow*. Considered immaterial, this cost is charged off in the period of issue as a bond interest expense and is not amortized over the life of the loan. The fixed fee is not incorporated into the estimated yield on bonds found in the Summary Sheet's section on "Rates on funding in quarter x."
- Bonds can be retired before maturity. They are callable at the bond call premium rate of 8 percent specified on the Summary Sheet. The call premium is treated as a current-period financial expense and is listed on the Performance Report under the line item "bond redemption costs." The most distant bond payment installments are retired first. As with the intermediate debt, the quarterly payments of different original bond issues coming due in a given quarter are aggregated. Thus, there is no way to retire a particular issue, and a part of the entire portfolio of bonds is called when a retirement occurs.

Example.   If $1,000,000 of bonds were to be redeemed by the company before maturity, the *cash outflow* would be the principal repayment of $1,000,000 plus the call premium of $80,000 (or $1,000,000 × 0.08).

- The *cash outflow* from bonds includes
  a. The quarterly interest, plus
  b. The principal repayment installment listed on the Summary Sheet, plus
  c. The first quarterly installment of a new issue of long-term debt or
  d. The dollar amount of prepayment on bonds plus the redemption cost of the payment.
- The four nearest quarterly installments on bonds are listed on the Summary Sheet and are considered a current liability on the Position Statement. Installments in the more distant future are aggregated in the bonds account. (See Exhibit 4.10.) The size and date of all the installments for the bonds due in periods beyond those shown on the Summary Sheet are $300,000 for quarters 5 through 9.

EXHIBIT 4.10   Bond Retirement Schedule

	Period					
	5	6	7	8	9	*After 9*
Payment (000)	$300	$300	$300	$300	$300	$0

Accounting Impacts.   The company issues $2,400,000 of bonds and $2,000,000 of two-year debt for quarter 2. The impact on all bond-related activities is included.

Cash Budget—inflow (issuance)		$2,400,000
Cash Budget—outflows:		
Flotation cost		50,000
New bond installment ($2,400,000/40)	60,000	
Prior bond installment	300,000	
Bond interest (on prior bonds from Exhibit 4.3)		33,600
Interest on new bond ([1.754% + 4 × 0.125%] × $2,400,000)		54,096
Performance Report—bond interest ($33,600 + $54,096 + 50,000)		137,696
Position Statement—bonds maturing:		
Prior bonds ($300,000 × 4)	$1,200,000	
New bonds (4 × $60,000)	240,000	1,440,000
Position Statement—long-term liabilities:		
Old bonds (3 × $300,000 [qtrs. 7–9])		$ 900,000
New bonds (35 × $60,000 [qtrs. 7–41])	$2,100,000	3,000,000

Decision: Long-Term Loan.   The long-term bond decision is entered on the Pro Forma Decision Sheet input form (see Chapter 2). Bonds can be either issued or retired before maturity each quarter. *A minus sign immediately preceding the dollar size indicates a call on the bonds before maturity.* All financing decisions are automatically reset to zero for each new set of quarterly decisions. The status quo is to have no financing; an active decision is required by managers to issue any new financing by entering the amount of financing desired each quarter.

Taxes

- The tax rate is constant throughout the game unless changed by the instructor.
- The percent rate is given in the Performance Report on the income tax line.
- The items that affect changes in taxable income are given in the Performance Report.
- Taxes are a *cash outflow* in the quarter they accrue and are automatically paid.
- It is assumed that there is always enough income earned in previous periods to utilize the benefits of any income loss carrybacks. A current-period negative figure for income before taxes will automatically generate a tax rebate equal to the tax rate times the loss. This is a current-quarter *cash inflow*.

Example.   Assume the firm represented in Exhibits 4.1, 4.2, and 4.3 had an income-before-taxes loss of $1,000,000 for the quarter. The tax rebate would be $400,000 (or 0.4 × $1,000,000).

Decision.   No active decision is required by the manager.

Equities

Common stock and preferred stock provide equity capital in the game. Here are the rules and conditions applying to outstanding equities and both the repurchase and issuance of equities.

Preferred Stock

Preferred stock is a fixed-cost, permanent-equity security. The preferred stock in the game has many conditions found with actual preferred stocks.

- The preferred stock required yield is derived in much the same manner as debt costs. The economic condition and the risk of nonpayment of preferred dividends enter into the determination of yield.
- Preferred stock is perpetual; once issued, it remains outstanding until repurchased. The dividend on the preferred is at a constant rate of $1.00 per quarter.
- The market price of a preferred stock is found by capitalizing the dividend by the required return rate on preferred stock.

Example.   The preferred stock price for quarter 1 would be $32.15 (or $1.00/.03110). The price for quarter 2 will be $38.17 (or $1.00/.0262). The yield rates are both presented on the Summary Sheet.

- Preferred dividends are automatically paid every quarter. The manager does not need to enter a decision for preferred dividends.
- Preferred stock issues or repurchases occur at the beginning of the quarter, and dividends are paid on the shares outstanding at the end of the period.

Accounting Impacts.   The company has 200,000 shares of preferred stock outstanding.

Cash Budget—outflow	$200,000
Performance Report—preferred stock dividend ($1.00 × 200,000)	200,000
Position Statement—preferred stock is the same as in the prior quarter	

Decision.   Preferred dividends are automatically paid subject to the restrictions covered next.

Preferred Stock—Dividend Payment Restrictions.   Preferred dividends are cumulative. If the firm's profitability deteriorates too far, preferred dividends will not be paid. This occurs only if the next two conditions both apply:

- The total of operating income before extraordinary items plus penalty interest is not sufficient to meet the before-tax cost of preferred dividends.

Example.   Assume that in quarter 2, the company had operating income before extraordinary items of $36,000 and a penalty interest charge of $83,000. The operating income before extraordinary items and penalty interest would be $119,000. If the company had 30,000 shares of preferred outstanding, the before-tax cost of the preferred dividends at a 40 percent tax rate would be $50,000 [or $30,000/(1 − 0.4)]. Since this is less than the adjusted operating income of $119,000, the dividends would be paid. Alternatively, if 90,000 shares were outstanding, the before-tax cost of dividends of $150,000 exceeds the $119,000 limit and no preferred dividend would be paid in quarter 2.

- The company has short-, intermediate-, or long-term debt outstanding during the quarter. The requirement that a firm not pay dividends in a poor profitability situation is often written into the debt contracts or indentures.

Disallowed current quarterly preferred dividends will be added to previous cumulative unpaid dividends. As soon as the dividend restriction conditions are withdrawn, all unpaid cumulative past dividends are paid. *Preferred stock can be neither issued nor repurchased if there are any outstanding unpaid preferred dividends.* Information on cumulative unpaid dividends is presented on the Summary Sheet account "Unpaid preferred dividend/share."

Accounting Impacts.   The company has 200,000 shares of preferred stock outstanding and dividends on preferred stock are disallowed.

Cash Budget—outflow	$0
Performance Report—preferred stock dividend ($0.0 × 200,000)	0
Position Statement—preferred stock balance is the same as in the prior quarter	

Decision.   Restrictions are automatically imposed when the appropriate conditions apply.

Issuance of Preferred Stock.   Preferred stock can be issued in any quarter to provide new external funds unless issuance, indicated above, is denied.

- Preferred stock will be sold to the public at the next quarter's market value. Flotation costs would be incurred and the full market value per share would not be received by the firm. There are three components to preferred stock flotation costs:

  a. A fixed fee per offering of $50,000 is charged.

  b. Two percent of the market value of the shares offered is charged as an additional discount.

  c. The receipts per share are inversely related to the size of the offering.

Example.   If the company issued 100,000 shares in period 2, its net receipts might be $3,537,980 [or ($38.17 × 100,000 × 0.94) − $50,000], where the size of offering premium is estimated to require an additional 4 percent discount over the standard 2 percent discount (and thereby a multiplier of 0.94). The $3,537,980 would be the amount added to the preferred stock account.

- The net receipts are added to the previous balance in the preferred stock account that appears on the Position Statement.

Accounting Impacts.   The company issues 100,000 shares in the above example and there are no prior preferred stocks outstanding.

Cash Budget—inflow	$3,537,980
Cash Budget—outflow (dividend)	100,000
Performance Report—preferred stock dividend ($1.00 × 100,000)	100,000
Position Statement—preferred stock	3,537,980

Warning: Large issues of preferred stock can require very substantial offering premiums. Preferred stock should be considered as a source for only a small proportion of needed external funds. It is not a reasonable substitute for primary permanent funds, which should come from common stock and long-term debt.

Decision: Shares of Preferred Stock.   Preferred stock is issued on the Pro Forma Decision Sheet input form (see Chapter 2). The number of total shares to be sold is entered on the form.

Preferred Stock Repurchases.   Preferred stock is repurchased either at a call price or at a current market price, whichever is lower. The call price per share is determined by multiplying the period's average book value per share times 1 plus a call premium. The call premium is constant throughout the game at 8 percent.

> **Examples.**   In the first case, the preferred stock account has a balance of $1,000,000 and there are 20,000 shares outstanding. The stock's market price in the period when it is to be purchased is $49.38. The book value per share from preferred is $50.00 (or $1,000,000/20,000). After adjustment for a call premium of 8 percent, the call price is $54.00 (or 1.08 × $50.00) per share. Since the current market value is lower than the call price, the shares would be purchased in open-market transactions at a cost of $49.38 per share.
>
> In the second case, the market price is assumed to be $56.00 per share and all other information is the same. The market price exceeds the call price of $54.00 and the shares will be called at $54.00 rather than repurchased in open-market transactions at a cost of $56.00 per share.

The difference between the average book value per share and the repurchase price is transferred to the common stock account.

> **Examples.**   In the first case above, $.62 (or $50.00 – $49.38) per share is credited to (or increases) the common stock account. In the second case, Times –$4.00 (or $50.00 – $54.00) per share is charged to (or decreases) the common stock account. In the game, the common stock account is used as a catchall for special owner equity accounts that affect common shareholder book value.

Accounting Impacts.   The company retires the 20,000 shares in the above example and there are no other preferred stocks outstanding. The market price of the preferred stock is $56.00 per share and the shares are called at $54.00 per share.

Cash Budget—outflow ($54.00 × 20,000)	$1,080,000
Cash Budget—outflow (dividend)	0
Performance Report—preferred stock dividend	0
Position Statement—preferred stock (None now outstanding)	0
Position Statement—common stock ([$50.00 – $54.00] × 20,000)	decreases $80,000

A preferred stock repurchase will be disallowed if there are any cumulative unpaid preferred dividends outstanding or the debt to total equity ratio is greater than 4 to 1. Short-term loans, intermediate-term loans, long-term debt, and penalty loans are the liability items used in the calculation. Restrictions of this type are usually found in debt contracts, called indentures.

Decision: Shares of Preferred Stock.   Preferred stock is repurchased and retired on the Pro Forma Decision Sheet input form (see Chapter 2). The number of total shares to be sold is entered on the form. A repurchase is distinguished from a sale by placing a minus sign before the number of shares if a repurchase is to occur. Therefore, a sale and repurchase cannot occur in the same period.

Common Stock

Valuation of Common Stock.   Common stock value is affected by six items. The first two items are measures of company expected earnings while the remaining four factors affect the rate of return required by shareholders on earnings.

- The total common stock value of the company is positively related to the anticipated *future level of earnings* to common stockholders. The current earnings to common stockholders given in the Performance Report are used as a starting point. Models internal to the game adjust for anticipated changes in future earnings.

  Example.   Excess inventories would lead to lower future earnings that may not yet be fully represented in current and historical earnings. Insufficient machine or plant capacity would also lead to anticipated future poorer performance, relative to firms with adequate capacities.

- The historical *growth rate of earnings* is also positively related to the firm value. A high-growth-oriented company has a higher stock value than a lower-growth company.
- The *economic environment* affects costs. In an expanding economy, both inflation and tightening by the Federal Reserve cause higher rates of return. The reverse condition holds with an expected downturn in the economy.
- Shareholders require a *risk premium* for operating and financial leverage. Within the firm, the probability of erosion of original investment increases as both forms of leverage increase. Outside the firm, the market price volatility of the shares would also increase. This would imply increased risk of losses to shareholders.
- The *dividend payout rate* affects common stock price. The optimal payout rate is inversely related to the earnings growth rate of the firm. A company with an increasing EPS should have a lower payout rate than one with a constant or declining EPS. In the game, the payout rate is calculated using the sum of the current and the last three quarters' dividends per share over the sum of the same quarter's earnings per share (EPS). The four-quarter average is used to decrease the effects of seasonal variations on the optimal payout policy.
- The *stability of dividends* also affects the shareholders' required rate of return. Stability, as defined in the game, exists when there are no decreases in the dollar dividends paid per share. Two items affect the importance of the stability policy.
  - *a.* The further the firm's actual dividend payout policy is from its optimal level, the smaller the effect of stability on cost.
  - *b.* As the EPS growth rate increases, the effect of dividend stability on cost decreases.

The value of common stock is modified by the above items in each period.

Manager Objective.   Managers should be able to minimize the overall cost of funds for their company. One of the manager's prime responsibilities is to form strategies that will lead the firm toward the objective of minimizing costs and maximizing the wealth of the common stock investors. See Chapter 3 for further discussion on strategy formation.

Issuance of Common Stock.   New shares of common stock can be issued. They are offered through an investment banker. Three items affect the divergence between the current quarter's closing share price ($35.57 in quarter 1, for example) and the per-share receipts from a new offering:

- There is a $50,000 fixed cost per offering.
- Five percent of the current market value of the share offered is charged as a flotation cost.
- The amount of receipts per share is inversely related to the size of the offering while receipts are positively related to reduction in uncertainty that can come from a less financially leveraged company.

The model providing an estimate of the actual receipts per share, *R*, includes all three of the above effects:

$$R = \frac{P}{1.05 + .5 S_n / S_o} - \frac{\$50,000}{S_n}$$

where

P = Current common stock price
S_n = Number of shares offered
S_o = Number of shares currently outstanding

The first component of the right side of the equation discounts the current common stock price by 5 percent to adjust for flotation costs. This component also includes a function, $0.5 S_n / S_o$, that makes the receipts per share, *R*, inversely related to the size of the offering.

- The number of shares to be issued must also be determined.
- The firm receives a current period *cash inflow* equal to the number of new shares issued times the receipts per share price.
- Common stock is no par. The full value of any issue goes into the account labeled common stock.
- The receipts per share figure is listed on the Summary Sheet under the heading "Common tender of sell/share." The line item has a zero balance when neither an offering nor a repurchase is entered.

Example.   In quarter 2, if the manager were to issue an offering of 100,000 shares, the receipts per share would be estimated to be

$$R = \frac{\$35.57}{1.05 + .5(100,000 / 1,000,000)} - \frac{\$50,000}{100,000}$$

$$= \$31.836$$

In the company's view, it could issue 100,000 shares with per-share proceeds of $31.836 and total proceeds to the company of $3,183,600 (or 100,000 × $31.836).

Accounting Impacts.   For the issuance just covered and assuming a dividend of 10 cents,

Cash Budget—inflow	$ 3,183,600
Cash Budget—outflow ($0.10 × 1,100,000)	110,000
Performance Report—common stock dividend ($0.10 × 1,100,000)	110,000
Position Statement—common stock ($8,000,000 + $3,183,600)	11,183,600

Manager Objective.   An optimal decision should be based on the firm's funding requirements, the capital structure, and the effect on proceeds of both the fixed cost and the size of offering. For more detail on optimal equity positions, see Chapter 3.

Decision: Shares of Common Stock Issuance.   The number of shares to be issued is entered on the Pro Forma Decision Sheet input form (see Chapter 2). The sales per-unit price is required in the "common tender price" decision input only for pro forma statements.

Repurchase of Common Stock.   Common stock repurchase is obtained through a tender offer. More information on the tender decision is covered in Chapter 5. The following conditions apply:

- The manager must establish the tender price per share that he or she is willing to offer for the repurchase of common stock. It is the manager's responsibility to determine the markup needed to successfully tender shares.
- The manager must specify the number of shares to be tendered. The repurchase price will be directly related to the size of the tender offer. The tender price is derived from the closing quarterly common stock price.
- The percent premium is also inversely related to the dollar value of a share, with a lower-price share having a higher-percent premium.
- The tender is exercised and the numbers of shares requested are repurchased if the tender price entered by the manager exceeds the demand-adjusted market price determined within the program.
- If the adjusted market price for the number of shares demanded exceeds the tender price, the shares that are offered by investors at the tender price are repurchased. This will be less than the number of shares requested. Managers do not have the real-world option of refusing the tender of any shares if the original number of shares requested is not forwarded by shareholders. Thus, an "all or none" option on the repurchase of common stock is not available.
- If the full tender is successful, the shares are repurchased at the manager's tender price, not at the internally computer-generated acceptable market price, which may be lower. Partially successful tender offers are also repurchased at the tender price, which is equal to the underlying computer-generated repurchase price.
- The total tender price of the shares actually repurchased is a *cash outflow* in the quarter that the tender is made.
- An after-tax cost of $1.00 is charged per share originally requested in the tender offer but not sold by investors to the company at the tender price. This charge is a *cash outflow* in the period the tender occurs. In a real situation, this would cover the advertising, legal, and other costs of a partially unsuccessful tender. This cost is charged against the after-tax income in the period of occurrence. The line item is given on the Performance Report only when the actual number of shares tendered is less than the original number sought.
- Repurchased shares can affect both the common stock and retained earnings accounts. The repurchase price is allocated to the accounts according to the weights in each of the accounts as a percentage of total common stock and retained earnings.

- A tender offer will be entirely disallowed for any one of three reasons:
  - *a.* If there are any outstanding unpaid preferred dividends in the most recent closing quarterly statements, repurchase is not allowed.
  - *b.* If the retirement would result in a negative equity balance in the previous period's common stock accounts, repurchase is disallowed.

Example. If a tender was made in quarter 2 and the tender price times the shares tendered equaled $12,000,000, this balance when netted from Period 1's retained earnings and common stock balance, $11,190,575 (or $8,000,000 + $3,190,575), would cause a negative common equity account balance. The entire tender offer would be rejected in this case.

  - *c.* The book-value debt-to-common equity ratio must not deteriorate below 4 to 1. This condition does not apply to the issuance of debt; it applies only to common stock repurchase.

Common stock issuance and retirement only temporarily have a direct effect on the common stock price. The tender price or issuance price causes the market price to increase or decrease only in response to the specific tender or offer size. This market response does not directly affect further quarterly closing prices, including the quarter closing price in the period a tender or offer takes place. The tender or issuance of stock can indirectly affect end-of-current-quarter and future common stock prices through the six common stock valuation conditions given previously.

Example. If 100,000 shares were tendered at $40.00 per share in quarter 2, the $4,000,000 (or $40 × 100,000) would reduce the common stock account by $2,859,526 {or $4,000,000 × [$8,000,000/($8,000,000 + $3,190,664)]}, and the retained earnings account would be reduced by $1,140,474 {or $4,000,000 × [$3,190,664/($8,000,000 + $3,190,664)]}. Additionally, the number of shares outstanding would be reduced to 900,000 (or 1,000,000 – 100,000) in quarter 2. The repurchase is treated as a retirement of stock.

Accounting Impacts.   The company retires the 100,000 shares in the above example and has a 10-cent dividend.

Cash Budget—outflow ($40.00 × 100,000)	$4,000,000
Cash Budget—outflow (dividend of $0.10 × 900,000)	90,000
Performance Report—common stock dividend ($0.10 × 900,000)	90,000
Position Statement—common stock ($8,000,000 – $2,859,526)	5,140,474
Position Statement—retained earnings	decreases 1,140,474

Decision: Common Stock Repurchases.   The number of shares management desires to repurchase is entered on the Pro Forma Decision Sheet input form (see Chapter 2). To differentiate a purchase from an issue, a minus immediately precedes the number of shares the manager desires to repurchase. A common tender price is also entered on the Pro Forma Decision Sheet input form to indicate the manager's per share tender price.

Common Stock Dividends.   Managers have the ability to issue dividends each quarter in the game. Any of the following conditions will result in an automatic decrease or elimination of dividends on common stock.

- If either loans or preferred stock is outstanding, the total common stock dividend of a given quarter will not be allowed to exceed the average quarterly earnings to common stockholders of the current and past three quarters.

Example.   The average earnings per quarter will be $400,000 if in the past four quarters the company's common stockholders have earned $300,000, $350,000, $400,000, and $550,000, respectively. If either loans or preferred stock are also outstanding in the current quarter, the total common stock dividend cannot exceed $400,000. With 1,000,000 shares outstanding, a management-declared dividend of 50 cents would automatically be reduced to 40 cents (or $400,000/ 1,000,000).

- If loans and preferred stock are outstanding and dividends on preferred stock are disallowed, then dividends on common stock will be disallowed.
- Dividend payments to common stock cannot exceed the total available ending-period retained earnings and common stock balances. Alternatively stated, dividends cannot cause a negative common stockholder equity position in the company.

Explanations for the above rules are given in Chapter 5. Rules similar to these are often required by state law, corporate bylaws, and debt indentures.

Dividends are a *cash outflow* in the quarter they are declared.

Accounting Impacts.   The company has a 10-cent dividend.

Cash Budget—outflow ($0.10 × 1,000,000)	$100,000
Performance Report—common stock dividend	100,000

Manager Objective.   A dividend policy needs to be developed that considers both optimal dividend payment level and dividend stability. Optimal policies are covered in Chapter 3.

Decision: Cash Dividends on Common Stock.   The dividends are declared quarterly on a per share basis in dollars and cents. The decision is entered on the Pro Forma Decision Sheet input form (see Chapter 2).

Performance Information

Performance information on the firm is available every period. In the game, as in the real world, the earnings information on the Performance Report gives one possible measure of the short-run success of the firm. In both the game and the real world, the measure is a relative one; it depends on the economic environment, the past asset and capital structure of the firm, the past earnings rate of the firm, and the relative performance of other companies.

To enable further comparisons, the following performance measures are reported in FG. More information on each item is presented in Chapter 5. All of the measures that follow are presented each quarter on the Summary Sheet.

Accumulated Wealth

Accumulated wealth is an overall performance measure for the firm. It includes:

1. The price of one common share.
2. The accumulated previously paid out dividends of one share of stock.
3. An external investment return on the previously paid dividends.

The assumption is adopted that common stockholders invest dividends they receive from the firm in other investments (external to the company) that return, on a quarterly basis, 1.5 percent plus the yield on risk-free marketable securities.

> **Example.**   From the yield rate in quarter 1, any previously paid out dividends would have earned a 2.862 percent (1.5% + 1.362%) return in quarter 1. This new balance, added to the dividend payments in quarter 1, would earn 2.862 percent in quarter 2, provided that the yield on marketable securities remained unchanged.

The accumulated wealth figure indicates better than any other single item the relative wealth position of the original stockholder. It is also the best single item for ranking the performance of the different firms playing the game. This holds since the price-per-share component is forward looking and incorporates expected future market conditions and company growth as in the real world. The other measures in FG are primarily historical performance measures; thereby, they are less informative.

Quarterly Earnings

The per share common stock earnings for the current quarter appear on the summary sheet under the title "Quarterly EPS." Income after taxes less preferred dividends and the stock tender costs is divided by the number of shares outstanding at the end of the quarter. The item can be used to estimate short-term relative performance by comparison either with the firm's previous quarters' EPS or with other firms' current quarterly earnings figures.

Dividend Yield

The dividend yield is an annualized yield based on the current quarter's dividend payment. This is derived by multiplying the current quarterly dividend per share by 4 and dividing the sum by the current price of the stock.

Investors tend to view the dividend yield as being important if the firm faces little growth potential. It also provides information for the dividend payout and stability decision. Normally, the dividend yield should not be used as a reliable measure of performance.

Price-Earnings Ratio

The price-earnings (P/E) ratio is calculated by dividing the common share price by four times the current quarter's earnings per share. "N/A" is shown in the P/E output field when earnings are negative.

Referred to as the *P/E multiple,* the price-earnings ratio is used by many investors as a rough indicator of investors' acceptance of the performance of the firm. A high multiple relative to other firms in the same industry indicates that the firm either is a relatively safe investment or faces better prospects for maintaining an earnings per share (EPS) growth rate greater than other related firms.

Although it is probably a better measure of performance than dividend yield, the P/E multiple is not without weakness as a performance measure. Chapter 5 evaluates this measure in more detail.

Return on Investment (ROI)

Return on investment (ROI) is a measure of return on total net assets. The current quarterly earnings after taxes from the Performance Report is annualized, by multiplying by 4, and divided by the total assets listed on the Position Statement.

The figure indicates the earning power of the dollar investment in the firm. The measure uses book values and thus fails to incorporate shareholders' views of the quality of the earnings. Thus, a firm with the highest ROI is not necessarily the best.

Return on Equity (ROE)

Return on equity (ROE) is an annualized measure of return on the total equity investment. The value of total equity from the position statement is divided into four times the current quarterly earnings after taxes. The earning power of a dollar of equity capital is thus obtained.

Many distortions that can occur with the use of either ROI or ROE in the real world are missing or limited in the game. Therefore, use of these items as short-term measures of relative historical performance is much more acceptable in the game than in a real situation. Chapter 5 gives reasons for the real-world distortions.

Conclusions

For each period of play, the game participant is provided with a starting set of information including the position, performance, and summary statements. With this, plus the information in this chapter and Chapter 3, the game player has all the rules and information necessary to formulate a set of decisions each period. The process is continuous, with the FG manager receiving feedback on previous decisions each quarter and formulating new sets of decisions for the next quarter that are based on both past performance and new forecasted information.

The chapter did not describe how proper or wealth-maximizing decisions should be made. As covered in Chapters 1 and 3, financial management texts should be continually used by the game's decision maker as a source of information on correct financial procedures and techniques. Applying correct procedures will better a company's performance in the game over what would be obtained when either planned or wealth-maximizing procedures are not utilized.

QUICK REFERENCE SOURCE

Company and environment rules and the manager's decisions are listed in alphabetical order to create a quick reference source. Abbreviated descriptions plus page locations of more detailed descriptions are provided with each item. The nature of the information is based on the chapter location where:

- Chapter 2 contains the Decision Form where decisions are entered.
- Chapter 3 holds strategy formation information with respect to the decision or rule.
- Chapter 4 covers rules and conditions that affect the item and the item's impact on other company variables.
- Chapter 5 compares rules affecting the item contrasting the game and the actual environment.

Advertising

Advertising has a positive impact on quantity demanded. The cost is a current-period expense included in the selling and administrative expense account and is a current-period cash outflow.

DECISION SCREEN, page 15. The prior-quarter entry is retained for the next-quarter decision form. See Chapter 3, page 34; Chapter 4, page 64; Chapter 5, page 101.

Capital Budgeting Projects

Different new projects A and B are available for purchase each quarter. The projects are independent within and among quarters. Either or both can be accepted or rejected each quarter. Projects affect overhead costs and direct labor costs. The *Summary Sheet* indicates the exact effects of each project every quarter. The cost is a current quarterly cash outflow. Projects are depreciated straight-line and depreciate even if not fully utilized. Projects become operational in the quarter purchased and immediately affect overhead and direct labor costs. Projects *do not* change the machine or plant capacity.

DECISION SCREEN, page 15. A new entry is required separately for a project A and/or a project B on each quarter's decision form. See Chapter 3, page 24; Chapter 4, pages 60–62; Chapter 5, page 101.

Cash Flows from Product Sales

Cash inflows on 33 percent of current quarterly sales are obtained in the current quarter. Accounts receivable are equal to 67 percent of sales and are all a cash collection in the following quarter.

DECISION: Effects are automatically performed by the simulation. See "Sales Discount," page 51, for generation of larger cash flows on current quarterly cash sales. See Chapter 4, pages 50–51; Chapter 5, page 97.

Cash Shortages and Marketable Securities Liquidation

If c is the cash shortage, the forced liquidation of short-term investments is equal to $1.03c$. The 3 percent forced liquidation fee is listed as "Financial Expenses: Penalty Loan Interest" on the Performance Report. Gross cash receipts therefore equal $(c\ 1.03)$.

DECISION: The liquidation of marketable securities is automatic when shortages occur. See Chapter 3, page 23; Chapter 4, page 53; and Chapter 5, pages 98 and 106.

Cash Shortages and Penalty Loans

See "Penalty Loan," page 54.

Common Stock

Value of common stock is affected by (1) earnings, (2) past and future estimated growth of earnings, (3) general level of business activity, (4) a risk premium on financial and operating leverage, (5) dividend payout, and (6) dividend stability.

New Issues.   New shares are issued with a $50,000 fixed flotation fee, 5 percent of current market-value variable cost, change in a risk adjustment premium, and size of offering premium. The formula giving the proceeds is on page 76.

Repurchase or Tender Offer.   Shares can also be repurchased through a tender offer. Managers must enter an estimate of the price required to repurchase the number of shares desired. The price required for a successful tender is based on the current market price on the most recent summary statement plus a premium that is directly related to the amount of stock being repurchased. If the tender price is insufficient for the number of shares desired, the shortage between the number of shares requested and the actual number tendered generates a $1.00 per-share tender cost, which is a current quarterly cash outflow. If the tender is successful, the shares actually tendered are retired following the rules on pages 77–79. See page 78 for reasons underlying the disavowal of a tender.

DECISION SCREEN, page 16. The number of shares is entered for an issue. The number of shares preceded by a negative number indicates a tender offer. The tender offer price is also entered on Screen 5. The values of both entries are reset to zero on the next actual quarterly Decision Form. See Chapter 3, pages 25–27; Chapter 4, pages 75–79; Chapter 5, pages 108–111.

Common Stock Dividends

Dividends are declared and paid quarterly on a per-share basis and require an active decision by managers each quarter. Dividends are disallowed if preferred dividends are in arrears. They are also limited or omitted if dividends either (1) exceed ending-period retained earnings and common stock balances, or (2) exceed the last four quarters' average earnings to common stockholders when either loans or preferred stock remain outstanding.

DECISION SCREEN, page 15. The dividends per share of common stock are entered in dollars and cents. The prior quarter entry is retained for the next quarter's Decision Form. See Chapter 3, page 27; Chapter 4, page 79; Chapter 5, page 108.

Debt Costs

Debt (percent) costs are determined by an underlying yield curve where rates are a function of the life of the obligation. The overall level of business activity is also positively related to interest rate levels, with a possible add-on premium for inflation. Company performance affects costs through risk premiums for the risk of insolvency. A temporary risk premium related to the size of the offering is also added to the rate. A premium is added equal to 0.125 percent per million dollars of total debt issued in a given quarter. See Chapter 3, page 25; Chapter 4, pages 66–70; Chapter 5, pages 102–107.

Direct Labor

The direct labor cost required to produce one unit of product varies for different unit volume production levels as indicated on the past quarterly *Summary Sheet*. New capital budgeting projects will decrease the per-unit direct labor cost shown on the *Summary Sheet* and must be considered in accurately specifying direct labor costs. Cash outflows equal to 90 percent of labor costs are a current-period outflow, while 10 percent of labor costs are part of the quarterly ending accounts payable balance that are paid the following quarter.

DECISION: Direct labor costs are automatically recorded within the game; a specific management decision is not entered. See Chapter 3, page 24; Chapter 4, page 56.

Dividends

See "Preferred Stock," page 72; "Common Stock Dividends," page 78; and Chapter 5, page 108.

Extraordinary Loss or Gain

Initiated by the instructor, a cash flow equal to the extraordinary gain or loss occurs. The quarterly performance report contains the extraordinary effect. See Chapter 4, page 65; Chapter 5, page 117.

Fire

The fire eliminates a given percentage of the company's machine capacity and all ending inventory. Insurance is received on the value of the inventory. No insurance is received on the lost machinery. See Chapter 4, page 65; and Chapter 5, page 117.

Forced Liquidation of Marketable Securities or Short-Term Investments

See "Cash Shortages and Marketable Securities Liquidation," pages 54–55. See Chapter 3, page 23; Chapter 4, pages 53–55; and Chapter 5, pages 98–99.

Intermediate-Term Loans

These loans have a life of 8 or 12 quarters and are repaid in equal installments, with the first install-ment due in the quarter of issue. The basic interest rates for issues are on the *Summary Sheet*, with a premium required for the size of offering. (See "Loans and Debt Costs," page 66). A cash inflow equal to the issue size is received. An outflow equal to past issue installments (from the *Summary Sheet*), plus the initial installment on new issues, and interest on all outstanding balances (see pages 67–70) are paid each quarter. Retirement of installments beyond the currently due installment is permitted and must be added to the current-period cash outflow.

DECISION SCREEN, page 16. The dollar amount of debt to be issued (or with a leading minus sign for extra debt to be retired) is entered. The values of both two- and three-year loan entries are reset to zero on the next actual quarterly Decision Form. See Chapter 3, pages 25–27; Chapter 4, pages 68–69; Chapter 5, page 104.

Labor Strike

Initiated by the instructor, a one-period strike may occur without warning. If the strike occurs, pro-duction is halted for one quarter. Lost sales cannot be made up. If a warning of an impending strike is given, managers have the choice of paying increased labor costs of $6.00 per unit for a 30 percent chance of a strike. The strike can be avoided with a $15.00 per-unit labor cost increase. If no conces-sion is given, the likelihood of the strike is 60 percent. The labor cost increases are permanent.

DECISION SCREEN, page 15 when initiated. The options for no increase, a $6.00 increase, or a $15.00 increase only show on the screen if there is an impending strike. See Chapter 4, pages 64–65; and Chapter 5, page 117.

Long-Term Bonds

With a life of 10 years (40 quarters), long-term debt can be issued and will generate a current-period cash inflow equal to the issue size. The debt is retired in equal quarterly installments starting in the quarter of issue. The yield on new debt is on the *Summary Sheet,* and there must be a premium for total debt issues of $1,000,000 or more as indicated in "Loans and Debt Costs," page 66. A fixed flo-tation cost of $50,000 is also required on all issues and reduces cash proceeds from an issue by this amount. Bonds can be retired before maturity with an 8 percent call premium. See page 70. Cash out-flows per quarter are equal to the quarterly interest, plus the principal repayment listed on the *Sum-mary Sheet,* plus the first installment on a new issue or the prepayment (plus call premium) of an old issue retired before maturity.

DECISION SCREEN, page 16. New bonds are issued, or old bonds are retired with a leading minus sign with the "10-year bonds" Decision Form entry. The decision value is reset to zero on fu-ture quarterly Decision Forms (Screen 6). See Chapter 3, pages 25–27; Chapter 4, pages 70–71; Chapter 5, page 104.

Machinery

One unit of machinery is needed to produce one unit of product. Thus, actual production cannot ex-ceed machinery capacity for the given quarter. One quarter is required before machinery can be used for production. Machinery has an eight-quarter life and is depreciated straight-line. Per-unit machinery cost is on the **Summary Sheet** and is directly related to future product demand. A cash outflow occurs in the quarter of purchase. Machinery expires even if not used, and it cannot be resold.

DECISION SCREEN, page 15. Units of machine capacity to be purchased are entered on the Decision Form. The decision value is reset to zero on future quarterly Decision Forms. See Chapter 4, pages 58–59; Chapter 5, page 100.

Marketable Securities Investments

See "Short-Term Investments," pages 52–53.

Marketable Securities Liquidation

See "Cash Shortages and Marketable Securities Liquidation," pages 53–54.

Materials

One unit of material at a cost of $15 is required to produce one unit of product. Only materials needed for the actual-period production are purchased with 90 percent of the cost being a current quarterly cash outflow. Accounts payable contains 10 percent of current quarterly material purchases and is paid in the following quarter. Inflation will cause material price increases.

DECISION: Materials are automatically purchased. Units purchased are equal to units of product produced. See Chapter 4, page 56; Chapter 5, page 99.

Other Overhead

A basic other overhead charge of $200,000 is levied each quarter. The other overhead charge can be changed by capital budgeting projects. The other overhead charge for each of the next four quarters (with no new capital budgeting projects) is contained on the **Summary Sheet**. A cash outflow of 90 percent of current charges occurs each period, with the remaining 10 percent being part of the ending accounts payable balance. This 10 percent is paid the following quarter. If plant and machine capacity are at zero units, no other overhead costs are charged.

DECISION: Overhead is automatically charged each quarter. See Chapter 4, page 62; Chapter 5, page 99.

Penalty Loan

A penalty loan is issued for end-of-quarter cash shortages that exist after the liquidation of short-term investments. The loan size is equal to the remaining cash shortage times 1.08. The .08 implies an 8 percent discounted note due in one quarter. Penalty debt is automatically retired in the following quarter with no additional interest charged.

DECISION: Automatic generation of the liquidation occurs when there is a cash shortage not covered by available marketable securities. See Chapter 3, page 23; Chapter 4, pages 54–55; and Chapter 5, page 106.

Plant

One unit of plant capacity is required to produce one unit of product. Thus, actual quarterly production cannot exceed plant capacity. Two quarters are required to build plant, which has a 20-quarter life and is depreciated straight-line once it is available for use. Plant expires whether or not it is used to produce units. The per-unit plant cost for the coming quarter is on the **Summary Sheet** and is directly related to future industry product demand. A fixed order cost of $250,000 is also added for each new plant capacity addition. A cash outflow equal to total plant cost occurs in the quarter of purchase. Plant cannot be resold or retired.

DECISION SCREEN, page 15. Units of plant production capacity to be purchased are entered on the Decision Form. The decision value is reset to zero on future quarterly Decision Forms. See Chapter 3, pages 29–33; Chapter 4, pages 57–58; Chapter 5, page 100.

Preferred Stock

Preferred stock is perpetual and requires a $1 quarterly dividend. New issues are at a price obtained by dividing the $1 dividend by the preferred stock rate on funding for the next quarter provided on the *Summary Sheet*. A fixed $50,000 offering fee, a 2 percent of market value fee, and both a change in risk premium and a size of offering premium must be considered in deriving estimates of the cash proceeds to the company. Dividends are cumulative if they cannot be paid. (See page 72 for details on initiating nonpayment.) Stock is repurchased at either the call price or market price, whichever is lower. (See pages 74–78 for details of repurchase.)

DECISION SCREEN, page 16. The number of shares to be issued or (with a leading minus sign) the number of shares to be retired is entered as the decision. The decision value is reset to zero on future quarterly Decision Forms. See Chapter 3, pages 25–27; Chapter 4, pages 72–74; Chapter 5, page 108.

Product Demanded

The quantity of product demanded is directly related to the general underlying level of economic activity. If "Unit Price of Product" is controlled, a higher price leads to decreased demand and a lower price leads to increased unit demand. Additionally, increased advertising leads to an increase in units of product demanded. No control of price and no advertising lead to a demand controlled solely by the economic activity level.

For affecting decisions, see "Advertising Costs," page 64, and "Manager Control of Product Pricing," pages 30–33. See Chapter 3, pages 29–33; Chapter 4, pages 47–49; Chapter 5, page 92.

Product Price and Demand Estimates

Future estimates for both price and demand on the *Summary Sheet* are generated randomly about the actual price and demand. The actual price and demand are used as the expected outcome in generating the estimates. Closer estimates are expected to be more accurate. More expensive forecasts are expected to be more accurate.

See "Purchase of Demand and Price Forecast," page 49, for the purchase of more accurate forecasts. See Chapter 3, pages 30–33; Chapter 4, pages 47–48; Chapter 5, pages 92 and 97.

Product Selling Price per-unit: Manager-Controlled

A unit demand greater (less) than the industry underlying actual demand is generated by the manager pricing units below (above) the industry price level.

DECISION SCREEN, page 15. Enter desired sales price. See Chapter 3, pages 30–33; Chapter 4, page 51.

Product Sold (Cash Flows)

Cash inflows on 33 percent of current quarterly sales are obtained in the current quarter. Accounts receivable equal 67 percent of sales and are all a cash collection in the following quarter.

See "Sales Discount," pages 51–52, for generation of larger cash flows on current quarterly cash sales. See Chapter 4, pages 50–51.

Product Sold (Units and Sales Revenue)

If sufficient production and inventory units are available, the units demanded will be sold. The product will be sold at the actual industry price if "Unit Price of Product" is not entered. If production and inventory are less than unit demand, sales are lost; back-ordering is not allowed.

See "Product Demanded and Sold," page 50, for units demanded. See "Manager Control of Product Pricing," page 51, for the impact of manager pricing. See "Purchase of Demand and Price Forecast," page 49, to estimate product price. See Chapter 4, pages 47–49; Chapter 5, page 96.

Product Unit Production

Machine and plant unit production capacity must both be at least equal to the production decision. If either capacity is less, the smaller of plant or machine capacity indicates the maximum possible production.

DECISION SCREEN, page 15. Enter the number of units to produce. If your entry exceeds available plant and machine capacity your decision will be decreased based on available capacity. See Chapter 3, page 29; Chapter 4, pages 57–58; Chapter 5, pages 99–101.

Production Costs

See specific items: "Materials," page 56; "Direct Labor," page 56; "Warehouse Fee," page 57; "Plant," page 57; "Machinery," page 58; "Capital Budgeting Projects," page 60; and "Other Overhead," page 62.

Purchase of Demand and Price Forecast

One set of demand and price estimates is generated for each of the next four quarters at no cost to the company. A second set of estimates of both demand and price is generated for four quarters for an additional cash flow and selling and administrative cost of $30,000. A third set is generated for an additional $45,000. Thus, all three forecasts are obtained for $75,000. More expensive forecasts and more recent forecasts are expected to be more accurate.

DECISION SCREEN, page 15. Select the "free," $30,000, or $75,000 forecast. The decision remains in effect for future quarters unless changed by the manager. See Chapter 4, pages 49–50.

Sales Discount on Receivables

The amount of current-period sales that are a current-quarter cash collection increases with higher discount rates. The sales discounted and collected with each discount policy are inversely related to economy-wide interest rates. With all discount policies, 67 percent of sales not discounted are collected in the following period. Revenues are reduced by the discount taken on sales that are collected in advance.

DECISION SCREEN, page 15. The appropriate option is selected for "none," "1%," or "2%" discount policy. The decision selected remains in effect for future quarters unless changed by the manager. See Chapter 3, page 28; and Chapter 4, pages 51–52.

Selling and Administrative Costs

A fixed cost of $1,000,000 plus 5 percent of quarterly sales revenue is levied and is a current quarter cash outflow. No charge is made when operating plant capacity is zero units. The costs of purchased demand forecasts, advertising, and an instructor-imposed penalty also enter the selling and administrative expense account. See also "Purchase of Demand and Price Forecast," page 49; and "Advertising," page 64.

DECISION: The fixed and variable costs are automatically included by the game. See Chapter 4, pages 63–64; Chapter 5, page 101.

Short-Term Investments

Short-term investments are for one quarter. Interest, capital gains, and capital losses on quarterly holdings are recognized each quarter. Revenues and cash flow are increased by interest receipts. Revenues and asset revaluation occur with capital gains, whereas negative revenues and asset devaluation arise from capital losses. Higher-risk short-term investments have higher expected returns but larger possible capital losses.

DECISION SCREEN, page 15. The amount of additional or new investment is entered. A leading negative sign indicates that a decrease in investment is to occur. Risk of short-term investment is also entered on the Decision Form with a value of "0" through "9" to indicate level of investment risk. Higher risk level numbers are for more risky investments. See Chapter 4, pages 52–53; Chapter 5, page 98.

Short-Term Loans

Issued for four quarters, short-term debt is retired in four equal installments starting with the current quarter. Retirement before maturity is not permitted. A new short-term rate is calculated each quarter and applied to any outstanding loan balances. Cash inflows equal to new loan issues are received. Cash outflows occur that are equal to 25 percent of the currently issued loan plus installments due from prior issues (presented on the **Summary Sheet**) and plus interest at the current prevailing rate on all outstanding loan balances.

DECISION SCREEN, page 16. A decision is entered only on new short-term loans to be issued. The decision entry is reset to zero on the next actual quarterly Decision Form. See Chapter 3, pages 25–27; Chapter 4, pages 67–68; Chapter 5, page 103.

Short-Term Penalty Loan

See "Cash Shortages and Short-Term Penalty Loans," pages 54–55.

DECISION: Automatic, no manager decision required. See Chapter 3, page 23; Chapter 4, pages 54–55; and Chapter 5, page 106.

Taxes

The income tax line of the Performance Report indicates the tax rate applicable to taxable income. Taxes are a cash outflow in the quarter accrued. If losses occur, there is a negative tax and a positive cash inflow equal to the negative tax.

DECISION: Taxes are automatically calculated and paid. See Chapter 4, page 71; Chapter 5, page 107.

Warehouse Fees

Warehouse fees are automatically recorded as a period expense and cash outflow each quarter. The fee is levied on the ending inventory at the rate of $1 per unit on the first 2,000 units, $3 on the next 4,000 units, and $8 per unit thereafter.

DECISION: Warehouse fees are automatically calculated and paid. See Chapter 4, page 57; Chapter 5, page 99.

CHAPTER

5

The Game and the Real World

Overview

FG companies operate in an environment that is similar to the operating environment of actual companies. Some of the game conditions described in Chapter 4 are unrealistic, and game participants should be aware of this. Game players also often believe that some FG conditions are unrealistic while these are commonly found in actual companies. To alleviate confusion, similarities and dissimilarities between the game and an actual operating environment are described. The material can also aid the FG manager in transferring, or envisioning how to transfer, knowledge gained from the game to an actual firm.

General Conditions

The major reasons for divergence between FG and an operating company's conditions and models are explained first. Some of the general environmental conditions outlined in Chapters 1 and 4 are examined for game and real-world differences. The second section of this chapter examines differences in conditions governing specific decisions, financial statement accounts, and performance.

Why Differences Exist

Some differences between the game and an actual environment exist by intention while others exist due to an inability to duplicate the real world. The intentional differences make the decision environment simpler so that FG managers can derive optimal decisions within the short time span and periods of play experienced in FG.

The Use of Simple Models

Using realistic highly complex multivariate models in a game would increase confusion and decrease effective learning. Consequently, the game is composed of a set of fairly simple models abstracted from the more realistic comprehensive models.

89

The more complete and complex multivariate models currently available in the fields of finance and economics are not used.

>   **Example.**   The Federal Reserve Board (Fed) might use a complex multivariate model, including possibly dozens of variables, to estimate future interest rates and judge how different Fed policies could affect interest rates. Incorporation of this same model in FG is feasible but not desirable. The game participants in 10 or 15 iterations could not be expected to derive the nature of the underlying model and use it to estimate the economy's impact on their companies' future interest rates, product demand, unit price and cost of machinery and plant.

Purposes and objectives of the game are achieved with less complex models, even though some degree of realism is sacrificed. The substantial number of security valuation, interest rate, price–demand, and cost functions in the game makes the decision requirements sufficiently complex.

Real-World Models—Difficult to Define

Actual underlying conditions are often too complex to define with any degree of confidence.

- *The number of variables that affect a given dependent variable might be very large*. The ability to specify a model is generally inversely related to the number of variables.

>   **Example.**   A company's interest rates are determined by fiscal and monetary policies, the business cycle, the geographic location of the firm, the industrial sector or sectors the firm operates in, the firm's operating and financial leverage, and a host of other contractual conditions imposed by different security and stakeholders.

- *Each relevant variable can have different lagged effects*. The complexity of the required explanatory model increases even more when conditions of a company are impacted from decisions made earlier in the company's life. The models can explode in size and complexity as all the possible relevant items are considered.

>   **Example.**   Money supply may have a lagged effect on interest rates. These rates could be affected by the money supply in each of the past 48 months. Each month's supply rate could have a different weighted effect on the interest rates. Whereas a simple model would have incorporated one variable for money supply, the more complex one would require 48 separate variables.

- *Many of the determining variables can affect the dependent variable in unanticipated and obscure ways*.

>   **Example.**   The total money supply might directly affect interest rates, while additional effects come from the percent rate of change in the money supply.

Adopting Theoretically Sound Models

The game has incorporated theoretically sound normative models where real-world models are unknown. The literature in finance includes numerous studies using actual data to test the soundness of theoretically derived models on the effect of company policies. Different studies have supported, rejected, or found inconclusive the proposed models.

Actual conditions are often difficult to duplicate in a game. FG adopts optimal debt leverage and dividend policy models.

Example.   Conflicting and therefore inconclusive evidence exists on the effect of financial leverage on a company's weighted cost of capital. Some studies have supported the assertion that leverage affects the firm's cost of capital, whereas other empirical studies have refuted the existence of an effect. If there were an effect, the firm's policy on financial leverage would affect both the cost of capital and the total value of the firm. The management planning function is increased when the assumption is adopted that financial leverage affects capital costs, and this is an assumption adopted by most managers. Thus, to increase the participant's exposure to decision making in as many areas as possible, FG adopts an interest rate model for debt and a valuation model for preferred and common stock that is affected by the firm's financial leverage position.

When there is a question in the literature on the choice of explanatory models, FG generally includes the normative model in which the concerned variables affect firm valuation. This is consistent with a major aim of the game to expose FG managers to the most comprehensive decision-making situation possible, given the constraints of both the iterations of play, the participant's time, and prior conditions on limiting the number of affecting variables.

Uncertainty in the Game

The degree and type of uncertainty in FG provide a decision-making environment quite like that of an actual firm. The greatest uncertainty in the game exists when play first commences.

Producing an Unknown Product

The FG manager is not familiar with the product the firm produces. With knowledge of the type of product—for example, fad-oriented toys or lightbulbs—managers could subjectively assess the reliability of the price and demand forecasts and anticipate the business risk of their firm. For planning purposes, this would decrease the relative uncertainty in the early iterations of the game.

The starting FG manager is given a firm not too unlike a new firm entering a new product area; little is known initially. The product is purposely undisclosed to prevent the game player from drawing on either rules of thumb or specific real-world industry data in initially estimating the reliability of the forecast data provided in the FG quarter 1 statements. No differential advantage is gained by managers seeking information outside the game manual. This requires the manager to focus on information in the quarter 1 statements to derive estimates of the type of product being produced.

The large initial uncertainty provides experience not easily obtained through other sources. The intent is to motivate the manager to find ways of rapidly securing further information to reduce uncertainty and, if necessary, to postpone decisions that might harm the company if there is insufficient information for a reasoned and sound decision. Thus, the game sacrifices some realism to increase demands on planning by the new manager. As the game progresses, managers gain knowledge of both the reliability of the forecast information and the nature of the firm's product. Uncertainty decreases and the game play comes closer to duplicating the decision environment in a real-world established company.

Uncertain Future Product Demand and Price

A continuing source of uncertainty in the game comes from the varying reliability of the forecasts. Each period's estimated future price and unit demand provide the manager with information used to establish machine and plant purchases and the size and timing of external funding.

Managers must judge the reliability of the forecasts and seek information on better forecasting.

The forecast of future prices and unit demand are given for the next four quarters on the FG quarterly Summary Sheet. This deviates from the practice of many actual firms, which project information much further into the future. Again, the nature of the product sold would dictate the relevance of projections over a more lengthy time period.

> **Example.** An electric utility company can anticipate quite accurately the increases in demand it will face for several years. On the other hand, a women's clothing manufacturer might have difficulty judging the market response to new garments offered in the coming quarter.

To enable the game to be reused over many semesters, it is purposely constructed to include forecasts with different degrees of reliability along with different price and demand patterns. The instructor can change the simulation to have an environment similar to that found in an electric utility company, a women's clothing manufacturer, or a firm somewhere between the two in terms of demand stability and certainty.

The confidence a manager can place in her decision is directly related to the forecast reliability.

> **Example.** A manager could justifiably have different responses to an expanded product demand estimate of 20,000 units. If estimates are accurate, and assuming profitability will be enhanced by sales of an additional 20,000 units, the decision to increase the amount of plant and machinery to meet estimates is justified. Alternatively, if estimates are subject to large error, the actual future demand might be very uncertain. The additional risk associated with the increased fixed costs of possibly idle capacity might encourage the manager to postpone expansion. The increases in risk might outweigh the potential gains from possibly larger sales and profits.

The manager must assess the reliability of the forecast information. A proper strategy places very little confidence in the estimates until their accuracy has been determined. In the game, the accuracy can be increased by the purchase of additional forecasts. After a number of iterations, the manager will gain increased knowledge about forecast reliability.

Forecasting in the game is not limited to the four-quarter projections provided each quarter. If the data were reliable and secular growth or a repetitive pattern of demand changes is evident, the manager might, after several forecasts and several periods of play, project demand and price estimates past the four periods of information provided. This could enhance the long-term planning function for the FG manager.

Operating Leverage and the Game

One approximation of business risk can be derived from the distribution of a company's possible operating profit outcomes. This distribution, in turn, will be derived from the firm's operating leverage, the volatility of product price, the unit demand, and the correlation between movements of product price and unit demand. All these items are primarily determined by the nature of the product being produced and only partially determined by management decisions.

The major items that affect the firm's operating leverage are not controlled by the FG manager. Unlike many actual managers, the FG manager has no choice of the product being produced. Game rules govern the amount and cost of the plant, machinery, materials, and other fixed and variable inputs required for production. Relatively minor changes in operating leverage can be affected by capital budgeting decisions.

> **Operating leverage comes from both the company's industry and management decisions.**

The amount of operating leverage is further influenced by the type of production scheduling used. Operating leverage will be greater for firms that maintain higher capacity levels to produce for maximum demand than for firms that either lose sales in peak demand periods or smooth production and meet peak demand with prior buildups in inventory. With respect to operating leverage, the FG manager must assume a role similar to that of a division manager. He cannot escape the possible problems of volatile earnings, low profitability, and lost liquidity by acquiring a new product line, changing businesses, or finding a new employer.

Financial Leverage and the Game

The risk of operating a firm is directly related to the amount of financial leverage the firm uses. This condition is completely controlled by the FG manager. By the issuance or retirement of debt and equity, the manager controls the company's financial leverage. Most of the conditions and rules that govern the various FG debt and equity securities are found in today's operating companies. The constraints on debt and equity placed on the operation of an FG company are generally less stringent than those found in many current companies.

Three restraints generally control the financial leverage of the firm:

- Many companies are kept from increasing financial leverage beyond a prescribed level due to limitations imposed by the debt holder. Debt indentures often specify a maximum debt ceiling and many other earnings and asset restrictions. The restrictions are imposed in an attempt to guarantee adequate interest and principal payments. The contract requirements attempt to protect debt holders from liquidating payments being made to equity holders while the debt holders' future claims will go unsatisfied.
- Specific company managers might be very risk-averse and arbitrarily restrain the firm from taking on judicious amounts of financial leverage. This policy could easily run counter to the wealth maximization of common stockholders if the company fails to have reasonable levels of debt given the operating risk position of the company.
- The shareholder clientele of the firm places restraints by requiring higher returns for their investment in highly leveraged firms. Beyond a point, the gains achieved by substituting lower-yield fixed-cost obligations for equity ownership are not sufficient to cover the shareholders' increasing risks. Beyond this point, increases in leverage will decrease common stockholder wealth.

> **Managers fully control the financial leverage of their company.**

When making decisions on financial leverage, the FG manager must consider how each financial leverage restraint affects the measures of firm performance. The risk aversion of the manager directly enters this process since both the average value and the variability of the performance measures are affected by this decision.

Constraints on Flexibility

Management options available in the game are more limited than options available to managers in many operating firms. The manager cannot change products, sell excess plant and machinery or stockpile excess materials or inventory in anticipation of price increases, control selling and administration costs, or negotiate loan covenants. These are only a few of the areas in which operating managers often have additional control that is not available in the FG firm. Thus, the game manager has less flexibility than an operating manager.

> **Example.** Assume a manager acquires an additional 20,000 units of plant capacity and then finds that the estimated unit demand projections were in error and the projected demand increase is not achieved. An actual firm might find a new market for the additional capacity by repricing the new output at a price exceeding the variable costs. Some contributions to the firm would be obtained even though the return might not match initial expectations. Alternatively, a decision might be made to abandon. The excess plant capacity could be sold immediately. Cash flows would be generated from both the sales value and the tax effect of any loss realized on the sale. As a third alternative, the plant capacity might be left temporarily idle in anticipation of future needs and/or leased. A manager could choose any of these alternatives or possibly a combination. The choice should maximize the position of the common stockholders. A present-value solutions would likely be needed to make the expected wealth-maximizing decision. This range of alternatives is not available to the FG manager. The abandonment alternative is not available. Repricing the entire firm's output is the only possible pricing alternative available.

Examples can be found in the real world that are quite similar to the somewhat restrictive environment of the FG manager. The rules of the game correspond to those of an actual firm where price discrimination is limited and where plant capacity is in a highly specialized area and might not have any resale value. The inherent risk attached to a given decision tends to be higher since the options available for cushioning losses are restricted in the game. The negative consequences of a poor decision are likely to be much more dramatic. Deliberate and careful planning is required to evaluate the risk-to-reward potential of all likely outcomes arising from a given decision.

Decision Requirements

Decisions must be made continuously in an operating company. FG decisions are made quarterly. With the mundane, but very necessary, daily requirements of an operating manager, it is easy to postpone, avoid, and forget to make the long-term decisions specifically required by the FG manager. If the material is in the wrong warehouse for today's production, a manager devotes time to this temporary problem rather than to next quarter's capital budgeting decisions. Day after day, the longer-term decisions are postponed or avoided.

The game reinforces the importance of long-term planning; it does not expose the game participant to the time-management solutions that encourage techniques and skills needed to jointly solve daily and long-term decisions.

In the real world, searching for financial information and preliminary analysis are important.

The likelihood of being locked into a given decision is greater in the game.

FG managers do not have the daily responsibilities that detract from long-term planning.

FG managers enter the decision process after information is already acquired.

Example.   With actual capital budgeting projects, costs, labor savings, and overhead cost effects are often not easily obtainable while they are given to FG managers. Changes in power consumption, insurance, parts inventory, material waste, and waste disposal are only a few of the items that need to be evaluated for possible inclusion in an actual project evaluation. None of this information is needed by the FG manager.

Decisions are made that require the following five steps:

1. Searching for initial information that affects a decision.
2. Determining the alternative decisions available.
3. Evaluating the alternatives.
4. Deriving the expected best solution.
5. Implementing the decision.

The emphasis in the game is on steps 3 and 4. In real conditions, step 1 and 2 activities are particularly important for proper firm management.

Game managers may gain the false idea that they have learned to properly manage all of a company while they actually have gained the ability to properly make decisions in only a few of the key stages of the decision process. Only limited experience is provided in the game in allocating scarce management skills efficiently to the different stages. Ability in this area often determines the quality of the manager.

Many companies practice the philosophy that only through experience in the firm can one learn how to make correct decisions for the firm. Partial justification for this comes from the requirements of stage 1, 2, and 5 activities. Success depends on an intimate knowledge of the specific firm's communication channels and information sources. A new manager often has difficulty making decisions because of both a lack of previous experiences in stages 1, 2, and 5 and a lack of knowledge of the specific information channels, rules, and conditions within the company.

The FG manager, even without stage 1 and 2 activities, is exposed to a fairly complex set of conditions. This information system must be mastered before the game manager can effectively make decisions in the firm. Barring the exceptions just provided, the FG manager makes decisions in a setting similar to an actual firm.

Informal Organizational Structure

The game does not directly incorporate the behavioral and interpersonal interaction effects among employees, customers, suppliers, and regulators critical to the successful operation of any organization. In operating firms, this has a comprehensive effect on the decisions.

Increased experience in decision making using interpersonal interaction can be obtained by having FG companies operated by teams of managers. The group must divide task assignments, compromise on decisions and work procedures, and establish its own peer, dominant, and subordinate relationships. These represent critical skills required by today's employers. Most real-world projects are managed by teams, often different teams for different components and stages of the project completion.

Even though it is a gaming situation, the amount of infighting and intra-group rivalry in FG might make one believe that the companies are real. Interaction has completely failed on a few occasions, and the firm has either stopped operation or continued with some of the managers ceasing to contribute. The failure to contribute was not due to a lack of knowledge or unwillingness to work; it was caused by attitude and personality conflicts. This experience highlights the dynamics of decision making when personal interaction is required in either the game or an actual operating environment.

Large and Small Businesses

The skills learned in the game are transferable to both large and small firms. Differences exist in specific financial instruments, account titles, input costs, and revenue sources.

> **Example.**   A small retail company will not have the options to obtain preferred stock and many of the types of debt available to an FG company. Coordinating the financial leverage of the firm with operating leverage and the risk preference of its owners is still required, even though financial leverage may have to come from short-term loans secured by receivables and inventories. The same capital budgeting techniques should be applied to a delivery truck replacement decision of a small firm or a $100 million plant for a large company. Even though the FG manager cannot issue commercial paper and equipment trust certificates, a correct strategy for managing the maturity term structure of liabilities is transferable to the large firm from FG.

Many specific skills needed to operate a given firm are not required in FG; they must be learned before a manager can successfully operate an actual firm. The objective of FG is to get the participant more prepared to enter a new and uncertain environment where much is unknown and must be learned very quickly.

Financial Statement Accounts and Performance

The remaining sections of this chapter describe the similarities and differences between the rules and types of costs, revenues, assets, and liabilities found in the game and in an actual operating firm. The material is presented in approximately the same order used to prepare financial statements. Income statement items precede coverage of balance sheet items. Performance measures are described last.

Revenues

As in most manufacturing companies, the major revenue-generating source in the game is from the sale of the finished product. A nominal source of income is from short-term investments.

Product Sales.   There are obvious differences between a one-product, one-market FG company and most operating companies. Few one-product firms exist today due to large and rapid changes in technology and consumer taste. High levels of diversifiable risk exist with a single-product firm due to product obsolescence rates being faster today than in the past. The ability of a one-product firm to adjust to rapidly changing environments is restricted. This risk is reduced in the multi-product firm where the company can respond to technological changes by shifting the mix of the products and constantly developing new products and product lines. The same risk-reduction techniques can be used to counter fads or shifts in demand.

Greater numbers and variations of marketing and sales options exist in the real world.

Many marketing and sales options used by firms are not available with an FG company:

- Managers cannot offer special services or divide customers into different groups to permit price discrimination and possible higher profits.
- FG does not allow product units to be withheld from sale to achieve expected holding, or windfall, gains from anticipated future price increases since units available for sale will always be used to meet product demand.
- *The pricing and unit supply of other FG firms do not affect the current or future price and unit demand of a specific firm.*
- Unlike many firms, no back-ordering is allowed in the game. Unfilled sales demand in a given period is not added to the following period's demand.

These conditions limit the marketing and product management decision-making requirements of the game to permit a greater concentration of effort on the financial decision variables. The product and market decisions are included in the game to provide the manager with some experience in recognizing the interdependence among financial and other functional area decisions of the firm. The conditions, however, do limit the ability to transfer decision skills gained from the production and marketing segments in FG to the real world.

Product Sales Estimation.   More accurate demand and price forecasts are generally available to a real company, provided the managers are willing to incur additional time and cost. The FG manager receives the first forecast automatically and can obtain two additional forecasts at higher costs.

In a real situation, the forecasts would be derived from forecasting models based on the general economy, specific lead indicators used in the industrial sector in which the manufacturer is producing, known product life cycle patterns, and possibly direct surveys. Forecast costs may be very substantial depending on the models chosen, the survey techniques and size, and the total data processing requirements.

Game managers have control over only the number of forecasts to be purchased. They cannot control the forecast techniques or the reliability of the forecast. Analysis and judgment are still needed in determining the value of the additional information. A net advantage will come from the difference between the incremental cost of a better forecast and reductions in inventory costs, better capacity usage, and decreases in sales opportunity losses. The analysis of the forecast purchase option needs to be performed regularly since the advantage gained from the additional forecasts can change over time. As game play progresses, the astute player will find lead indicators that provide better estimates than the most expensive forecast, thereby improving forecasting at lower costs and increasing performance relative to less capable managers.

Cash Flows from Product Sales.   Sales discounts are available to induce earlier payments of receivables. The discounts are used at the wholesale and occasionally the retail levels in many industries. A sales discount is the only accounts receivables policy controllable by an FG manager. The manager does not control the choice of credit customers, the use of quantity discounts, and other legal discriminatory pricing and collection policies that affect marketing and the finance function.

The discount does result in differences in quarterly sales collections and is, therefore, a determinant of the investment balance in accounts receivables. The

Sales discount policy
does not affect unit sales
in FG.

relationship is realistic to the extent that higher discounts increase receivables collection and decrease the company's investment in accounts receivable.

The effects of the receivables discount policy are somewhat unrealistic. In an actual situation, a change in discount policies often changes the sales demand. Sales demand is not affected by the discount policy in the game. The discount policy is also more flexible in the game. It can be changed quarterly and have no negative consequences on customer loyalty and unit sales levels. In a real-world situation, we would expect negative customer reaction to an uncertain and irregularly changing policy.

Marketable Securities.   The options available for the temporary investment of excess cash funds are fairly broad for the FG manager. In actual companies, the manager also has a host of possible temporary investment opportunities that enable shifts in both the portfolio's maturity structure and the risk of the underlying securities in the portfolio. All levels of government, special agencies, and private enterprise institutions offer securities of varying maturities. If a security that matures in 90 days is desired, Treasury bills, tax anticipation notes, commercial paper, or many other longer-term securities that have only 90 remaining days to maturity can be used. Both yield and risk vary depending on the financial soundness of the institution issuing or guaranteeing the security.

For either hedging or speculative reasons, the manager could hold a portfolio containing securities with a maturity either longer or shorter than the expected liquidation date of the portfolio. For example, if a manager speculates correctly that long-term interest rates will drop, price appreciation can be gained on long-term bonds purchased for a short-term period. For this reason, long-term bonds, preferred stock, and common stock of other companies are held in temporary investment portfolios by actual companies.

Short-term investment managers must manage the maturity structure, risk, and size of the portfolio. In the game, the size, timing, and risk of the short-term investment are management-controlled decisions. The proper management of temporary funds is stressed.

In FG the yields on short-term marketable securities are quite small relative to the profitability of the product-line investments and the cost of capital. Because of the advantageous profit opportunity of production over marketable securities, the best managers will make the more difficult production decisions and will achieve better performance measures than poorly managed firms that merely place excess funds in marketable securities.

Managers can obtain higher returns in the game by increasing the degree of risk in their short-term investments. The risk could be viewed as coming from selecting securities that have both more credit risk and a longer maturity. In an actual environment, managers can choose both maturity and credit risk with each security purchased, whereas in the game, separate control of the two determinants of risk is not available.

Realism is also lacking because managers cannot obtain longer-term capital gains from their holdings. The game automatically records capital gains and losses at the end of each quarter on short-term investment holdings. In an actual setting, managers could defer the recognition of capital gains or losses to the security sales date and thereby usually obtain a lower effective tax rate.

A penalty for forced liquidation of marketable securities, due to negative ending cash balances in the game, is consistent with what is found in an actual situation. Some large, face-value, short-term securities are not very marketable. For example, if managers must sell previously purchased tax anticipation notes before maturity, they will often find few buyers who want a note with an identical size, maturity date, and risk. This "thin-market" condition will necessitate a higher yield or a lower selling price, thereby imposing an additional penalty when forced liquidation is required. The game incorporates this penalty to encourage managers to better manage cash and marketable securities. Sound cash management would result in low cash balances, all excess cash invested in short-term marketable securities, and only an occasional forced liquidation of marketable securities and even less often the need for penalty loan financing.

Production Costs

The resources required for production are quite simple in FG. Unlike a multistage product that requires different materials, labor, and equipment at each stage of production, the product is produced in a single stage. The lack of emphasis on decision requirements of a nonfinancial nature is the reason for this simplification.

Materials, Labor, and Other Overhead Costs.   Early purchase of raw materials in anticipation of cost increases is not allowed in the game. Costs of materials, labor, and other overhead items are also not affected by product demand. Additionally, the manager has no control over cash outflows associated with materials, labor, and other overhead charges. In an actual firm, managers can often postpone cash outflows on some of these items and thus have greater flexibility in maintaining liquidity.

Labor costs per unit vary at different production levels. As production levels increase, the labor costs per unit decrease, first at 60,000 units and again at 100,000. The costs increase at 120,000 units. The underlying nature of the cost function is somewhat realistic. As production increases, fixed levels of employee wages are spread over a larger number of produced units. At high production levels, the costs increase as additional work shifts with less trained employees and higher overtime pay are necessary. The marginal productivity of labor then declines.

In some respects, the changes in labor costs are unlike those in an actual firm. Changes in costs per unit occur at specific per-unit volume levels in discrete, widely spaced steps. A more realistic portrayal might have labor costs decreasing as each additional unit is produced. At a turning point, per-unit cost would gradually increase. Realistic labor cost calculation requirements would be substantial if included in the game. On the other hand, labor contracts with guaranteed minimum hours, minimum overtime guarantees, and specified overtime rate requirements could cause the rate structure to be somewhat like the one used in the game.

Warehousing Fees.   The financing costs for investment in inventory, as well as the warehousing fees, are carrying costs that need to be considered in formulating production and inventory policies. Storage costs in the game are fully variable. As inventory increases, more expensive facilities or facilities that require greater handling expenses have to be used. A similar cost pattern might be found with a company that rents its needed warehousing space by the square foot. The cost patterns for many firms are quite different from the cost patterns in the game.

- A firm that maintains its own facilities would have fixed warehouse costs. On an average per-unit cost basis, the rate decreases initially as the fixed costs are spread over increasing numbers of units.

Single-stage production and a single product make FG planning much simpler than production in a real company.

- Warehousing costs are normally based on an average daily, monthly, or quarterly inventory base and not exclusively on the quarterly ending levels.
- Many inventory carrying costs are not addressed in FG. Insurance, breakage, spoilage, and obsolescence are not directly included. The warehousing fees could represent costs like the insurance component but not the wastage and spoilage costs since units of product are not lost in a FG company's inventory.

Machinery and Plant Costs.   As in the real world, the FG manager must maintain plant and machinery capacity levels adequate for the firm's production levels. Both expiration and increases in unit demand may warrant additional purchases of plant and machinery. There are several areas where the conditions that govern the FG firm can vary from conditions that affect a specific company or industry.

- Most actual companies have some variability in their production capacity level. With specific plant and machinery, an actual company might have a maximum capacity of between 90,000 and 110,000 units depending on varying conditions. Weather, employee attitudes, and slight variances in material quality can change the maximum capacity. FG companies have a constant maximum capacity. The game thus has a more certain environment with this factor of production.
- Management often has options on the lead-time requirements of capacity increases in plant and machinery. By either paying bonuses or receiving discounts, a manager can affect the lead time. No options are available in the game to adjust the two-quarter lead time for plant and the one-quarter lead time for machinery. Restrictions on lead time are found in actual situations to justify their use in the game.
- A cash outflow equivalent to the total purchase price of ordered machinery or plant is required in the game. An operating firm manager has many options from postponing payment until the machinery or plant is operating to obtaining percentage-of-completion loans that fund the actual cash outflows as they occur. The FG requirement is intentional. FG managers must actively control the liquidity of the firm while also making the capital structure decisions required when major replacement or expansion is occurring. The availability of specific funding packages attached to plant or machine purchases has a strong tendency to distract the manager from actively controlling the capital structure decision.
- One simplifying yet highly unrealistic condition in the game is that the depreciable life and the useful life of equipment and plant are identical. One unit of machine capacity can be used to produce one unit in each of the eight quarters of its useful and depreciable life. Most firms have buildings, machinery, and equipment operating from several periods to decades past their original depreciable life. This might not speak too well for the accepted accounting depreciation techniques, but it is found in nearly every firm. The game retains the restrictive assumption mainly to simplify both the rules for operating the game and the record keeping of the FG manager.
- Machinery and plant expire over time whether they are used or not. Nonuse does not postpone the expiration of machine potential. Technical obsolescence and wear that are a function of time rather than of use explain this condition in an actual firm. Automatic expiration through time is used

in the game to provide a larger penalty for overcapacity than would be the case if useful life were a function of units produced.

- Gains can be obtained by postponing tax payments. Accelerated depreciation methods are widely used by most firms to defer tax payments. The less advantageous straight-line method is used to minimize game complexity. This simplification decreases the manager's required bookkeeping calculations over the requirements of the accelerated depreciation techniques while also decreasing the NPV of any long-term acquisitions. The straight-line method is consistent with Generally Accepted Accounting Principles (GAAP) and gives rise to deferred income taxes payable as a liability. Thereby, companies have two sets of accounting "books," one for the tax purposes that report the actual tax cash flows and the other for GAAP, which tries to better match expenses and revenues over the long term. The simpler FG rule has the GAAP and tax "books" identical.

- Sale, abandonment, or removal before the end of the estimated useful life of plant and machinery is not allowed in the game.

The major rationale for the deviations between the game and actual operating conditions remain the same as enumerated either earlier in this chapter or in the discussions of specific conditions in Chapter 4.

Capital Budgeting Projects.   Capital budgeting projects generated in the game are sufficient to approximate very simple actual projects. There are few material differences between the projects in the game and the projects found in an actual firm. A few of the restrictive conditions just covered under plant and machinery also apply to the capital budgeting projects; these are not restated.

Decision-making requirements are often not obvious when presented in a complex, unfamiliar setting. Without previous explanation by the instructor, few prior game players have accurately estimated the projects' NPVs. Most quarterly sets of projects A and B should be evaluated as independent projects. Projects are independent for capital budgeting purposes when the acceptance of the second project does not affect changes in the expected cash flows of the first project evaluated. This leads to the condition where the decision of A is not dependent on either the acceptance or rejection of B.

Selling and Administrative Expenses

FG managers have very limited control of selling and administrative costs relative to a real company.

FG managers do not control most of their company's selling and administrative expenses. Managers have no control over policy in distribution channels, management centralization, and most other areas of the marketing and management functions.

Advertising

Managers do have control of the company's advertising expenses. The advertising expenditure represents an aggregate of separate decisions made in real companies. There is no control over establishing the characteristics of an advertising campaign. The mix of advertising mediums, from Internet and print to radio and TV and billboards, is not determined by the manager. Because the events that determine an advertising strategy are not under the control of the FG manager, the decision in the game is a financial variable optimization issue and not a marketing decision.

Financial Expenses

Proper management of the capital structure is a major determinant of common stockholders' accumulated wealth maximization in FG. A comprehensive knowledge of the rules that affect both equities and debt is necessary for successful decisions. The general rules affecting all debt items are evaluated. Next, the rules that affect specific debt items are examined.

Maturity and Debt Costs.   In the game, the required yield rate can be positively related, inversely related, or unrelated to the original life of the debt issue. The instructor controls the slope of the underlying yield curve and even may change the slope while the game is under way. If the inverse relationship between yields and maturities holds, a short-term loan requires a higher return than intermediate-term loans or long-term debt. This condition implies that the FG environment has a decreasing yield curve. A tight money policy of the Federal Reserve Board could cause a negatively sloped yield curve similar to the one incorporated into the game.

When a negatively sloped yield curve is used in the game, managers are rewarded for accepting both a decrease in flexibility and the increased planning requirements necessitated by accepting longer-maturity debt. The reward is in the form of expected lower interest costs for the same total amount of funding. A higher expected return will accrue to the residual equity holder. Not surprisingly, the basic tenant in finance holds that greater expected return, in this case from lower interest costs, brings greater risk. The longer-term debt commitment has greater risk since the future management options are reduced, unexpected interest rate decreases would lead to large opportunity losses, and refunding of the bonds with their high call premium can be costly.

> **Example.**   Assume an FG manager selects bonds over short-term securities for anticipated lower costs. Contrary to expectations, interest on all new debt items, including long-term bonds, decreases in the next period. The original decision results in committing the company to higher costs for 39 additional quarters. Alternatively, the high-cost bonds can be called at an 8 percent premium and a new, lower-cost issue authorized. In both alternatives, the company incurs substantially higher costs than would have been accepted if a shorter-term loan were originally used.

Managers need to consider the yield curve in determining the mix of the types of debt to use.

Rewards are consistent with maximum flexibility and greater liquidity management when a positively sloped yield curve is used. Larger short-term debt balances then increase the planning and management time required in continual debt-refunding requirements. Additionally, for a given level of outstanding debt, the per-period principal payments are larger with shorter maturity debt. A company with uncertain cash flows then has a greater insolvency risk. Since insolvency cannot occur in FG, instead very expensive new loans and low-priced stock would serve as the only means of replacing maturing debt that cannot be paid with internally generated cash flows. In extreme cases a $2 to $3 share price is not an uncommon outcome.

Debt Costs and the Business Cycle.   Interest costs are directly related to the general economic condition. The demand for investment funds is greater in an expanding economy than in an economic downturn. This tends to place upward pressure on all interest rates. To reflect this condition, an FG company's interest rates are also affected by an underlying economic indicator. This indicator also affects demand, the valuation of stock, and the cost of plant and machinery. As in an actual company, the manager must analyze and attempt to determine the relationship among interest rates, unit demand, unit price, machinery cost, plant cost, and interest rates. An ability to estimate future shifts in the firm's interest rates will also greatly enhance decisions relating to debt issuance, selection of debt maturity, issuance of equity and plant and machinery purchases.

Risk of Insolvency.   Two risk factors, defined in Chapter 4, are used to derive the yield premium for insolvency. The first factor estimates the firm's long-run ability to meet its debt commitments. The effect of this factor on risk premiums in FG and the real world needs to be constantly considered by managers. This condition indicates the importance of closely controlling the combination of operating and financial leverage in the game and in an actual firm. A firm evaluated as being very risky may have prohibitive interest rates of 5 percent or more per quarter. Not like in FG, in an actual situation, a very risky firm would be constrained from obtaining additional debt. The high possible rate in the game serves as a substitute for the actual world constraint. Other than being more sensitive, the insolvency factor's effect on yield is similar to the real-world effect.

The second factor adjusts for intra-quarter debt changes. Directly related to the size of a new offering, the factor would be found in an actual environment where there are thin markets or possibly high agency costs in obtaining external funds. In capital markets the size of the United States or Canada, no one company is so large that it causes a material shift in the market-wide rates of interest. The supply of one new security by even a corporate giant is not sufficient to cause a significant right-ward shift in the supply curve of securities and, thereby, an increase in the cost of funds.

For debt holders, an agency cost arises because of the possible wealth transfer from them to the managers or common stockholders. (See the "Common Stock" subsection later in this chapter for more information on agency costs and signaling effects.) This phenomenon explains the game's 0.125 percent size-of-offering premium per million dollars of each quarter's new external debt financing. Empirical evidence on this relationship of agency cost to the size of a debt offering holds when a company issues debt that substantially increases the company's financial leverage. In a similar example, home mortgage rates are an inverse function of the percent of equity used to finance the purchase.

The size of offering is often contrary to what is found with the usual debt issuances of an established company with a large debt offering if it does not substantially change the firm's financial leverage. Then the percentage of proceeds can increase as the offering size increases due to the spreading of fixed offering costs. This results in a slightly decreasing percent yield as offering size increases.

It is the manager's responsibility to estimate the relationship between the company's cost of each specific type of debt and each of the three yield determinants of maturity, business cycle, and risk of insolvency. This information should be used in first deriving and then adjusting both the maturity pattern and percentage of financial leverage used by the firm.

Short-Term Loans.   The loan is similar to a short-term bank loan repayable in four equal installments. Like a bank loan based on the prime rate, the interest rate charged on the outstanding loans in each period is derived from the current money market rates and the firm's risk of insolvency premium. The prime rate is for loans to firms with a very high credit standing. A firm with greater operating and/or financial risk than the highly rated firm must pay an additional premium.

An actual company would have some type of prepayment arrangement. Prepayment of the short-term loan is not available in FG. To limit confusion and complexity, commitment fees, compensating balances, subordination, collateral, and other contractual requirements often used by banks for a line of credit are not included in the game.

Intermediate-Term Debt.   The game's intermediate-term debt, usually referred to as *term debt,* is very similar to short-term debt except for the longer life of the loans and the ability to retire them before maturity without a penalty. Interest rates on intermediate-term debt vary from those on short-term notes in accordance with the conditions affecting yields specified earlier.

Term debt in a real-world situation is somewhat different from term debt in the game.

- Term debt generally is used to fund a specific project. In the game, there are no restrictions on the issuance of term debt. One new loan for each possible maturity can be issued each quarter, thus continually renewing earlier issues and providing a permanent source of funding that often is also found in a real environment.
- Collateral is commonly pledged for a term loan in a real situation especially for smaller capitalized companies. The game does not include a method of pledging assets or establishing collateral loans.
- The average yield on the remaining outstanding debt is not affected by retirement. In a real situation, the average yield might well be affected. A manager could specifically identify loans taken out in previous periods and retire those that most reduce interest costs.
- Retirements occur starting with the most current principal and including the most recent remaining installments in order.

Long-Term Bonds.   Long-term bonds have a 40-quarter life. The conditions that affect intermediate-term debt, covered in Chapter 4, also apply to bonds with the following exceptions:

- A call premium is required for the retirement of bonds, while there are no costs of retiring intermediate-term debt.
- The most distant payments are retired first, whereas the nearest future payment is retired first with intermediate-term debt.
- A fixed $50,000 flotation cost is charged for each bond offering. No fixed fees are charged for the issuance of intermediate-term debt.

These three conditions increase the planning requirements in bond decisions over the decision requirements of short- or intermediate-term debt.

Call Premium.   First, there is an additional charge for the option to retire a previous debt-offering decision by retiring the issue. The call premium determines this cost. The need to retire bonds can come from an overleveraged capital structure. Overleveraging may result from either a previous management error or a change in the operating risk of the firm. The shift in operating risk may be induced by either external environmental changes or internal firm management. An overleveraged capital structure problem can be rectified by debt retirement and/or equity offerings. The choice should be made after carefully considering the net operating funds needed by the company over the next several quarters.

Bond retirement can also be desirable if a substantial downward shift in interest rates has occurred. A replacement of the old bonds with new ones may be desirable if a change is not needed in either the percentage of financial leverage or the general maturity structure of the outstanding debt. With a refunding decision, the manager must determine and evaluate differences in cash flows and costs that will result if a refund is made. The proper NPV evaluation procedure is included in most introductory texts in finance.

Due to the input decision limitations of the game, both a repurchase and an issuance in the same period are not possible. If the manager wishes to refund debt, the debt will have to be retired in one period and new debt issued in the next period. A temporary source of external funds might be needed to cover the temporary reduction in total long-term debt. An intermediate-term debt would probably be best since it can be issued for the needed quarter and retired in the following period with no penalty charge.

The call feature is realistic since almost every bond indenture contains a call provision. The premium is fixed at 8 percent in the game. In a real situation, the call premium rate on new issues can vary depending on the financial position of the company, the relative level of debt interest rates, and the supply and demand of funds in the bond market. The call rate on a given actual bond usually declines in stated increments at specific points in time over the life of the bond.

Retirement of Principal.   The 40-quarter life of a bond substantially exceeds the number of periods the manager will play the game. Planning for cash management will be substantially reduced if retirement of bonds started with the most recent quarter.

> **Example.**   Assume a manager wishes to avoid the quarterly debt-funding decision. The first step would be to float a larger bond than necessary and then temporarily invest the excess in marketable securities or reduce term debt. In the following quarter, excess funds from the original offering would be used to retire the first 12 to 15 quarterly installments. For the rest of the game (12 to 15 quarters), the manager will not have to be concerned with quarterly debt payments. Payments will be effectively postponed until after the manager leaves the firm. This financing decision is especially desirable if interest rates are expected to increase materially. A longer duration debt issued at a low rate will have a greater opportunity wealth gain if interest rates increase.

The game does not reduce the need for refunding of prior bond installments since the most distant ones are retired first when a retirement is initiated. This condition is not applied with the term loans since their three-year maximum life falls within the manager's operating time horizon.

Fixed Flotation Fee.   The inclusion of a fixed flotation fee should lead a manager to consider applying an economic order quantity (EOQ) model in determining the issuance size and frequency of bond offerings. One clearly will not offer $10,000 in bonds in a quarter if there is a $50,000 cost just to have an offer. Actual flotation fees have underlying fixed- and variable-cost components. An actual manager's net proceeds per bond increase as the offering size increases. In the game, the size of offering premium is a variable-cost component; the debt's percent rate of interest implicitly includes this variable cost component based on the total debt offered in a quarter.

Other Bond Similarities and Differences.   Bonds in the game are similar to serial bonds. An issue contains bonds with several different maturity dates; they mature periodically until final maturity. The bond characteristics are not standard in a few minor respects. Most serial bonds have semiannual interest and principal repayments. The game uses a quarter of a year as the time increment. The FG bonds have a life of 10 years. Most general bonds have lives of from 20 to 30 years. The 10 years extend sufficiently beyond the manager's operating time horizon of 10 to 15 quarters so that a longer maturity is not necessary.

Debt conditions in the game are the same as an actual firm can have with privately placed debt. Intermediate debt can be repurchased at the option of the company at the issuance price. With bonds, the call premium must also be paid.

If the debt items were offered through a public offering, there would be an extra option not available in the game; the firm can repurchase its debt in the open market at currently prevailing prices. Thus, increasing market yields effect an increase in the company's debt yield rates, and the market price of the debt instruments can fall below the original issue price. If there is an adequate return for refunding or a need for decreasing financial leverage, there is an advantage in using open market purchases if interest rates have increased rather than using a call.

An option for allowing either open market purchases or a call, though not available with the various debt instruments, is available in FG with preferred stock repurchase.

In summary, managers in the game are responsible for determining the degree of financial leverage and the maturity structure of their firm's outstanding debt. The rules and conditions that specify both the general environment framework for debt and the specific types of debt are fairly realistic. The decision options available to the manager are similar to those found in an actual firm, although the manager does not obtain the experience with many of the specific conditions and options often faced in an actual company.

Short-Term Penalty Loans.   The short-term penalty loan is a special FG debt instrument that is not found in actual companies. Negative cash balances at the end of the FG quarter are first covered by liquidating marketable securities and next by the issuance of a penalty loan. The loan issuance can be either unplanned or planned. Unexpected events can cause the issuance of loans. The unexpected negative cash balance could come from faulty cash flow planning, unexpected increases in cash outflows, or unexpected decreases in cash inflows. By negatively affecting profitability, the penalty loan rewards accurate and penalizes poor cash flow management.

The use of the penalty loan can also be intentional. Rather than maintaining large permanent precautionary cash balances (at an average quarterly cost of the firm's cost of capital), the manager can intentionally ignore precautionary balances and rely on the penalty loan to supply funds when an unexpected negative balance occurs. The long-run cost might be less with the penalty-loan alternative. This depends primarily on the likelihood and size of possible negative balances. Also, the penalty loan can be a source of funds "of last resort." If the yield rates of other debt choices exceed the penalty-loan rate of 8 percent quarterly and equity prices are seriously depressed, the penalty loan can be a viable short-run source of funds.

Intra-quarter Cash Flows.   In a real firm, the manager has intra-period knowledge of cash inflows and outflows. A liquidity problem can be avoided by intra-period acquisition or investment of funds. The intra-period operations of FG are not like those of an actual firm. The maintenance of liquidity or cash solvency is the major difference.

Negative cash balances are not generally found in an operating firm; the cash inflows have to ensure the maintenance of positive cash balances every day. In the game, cash balances are checked only after all other quarterly transactions are recorded. If a negative cash balance then exists, a cash inflow offsetting the negative balance is generated by the issuance of a penalty loan. During the quarter, negative cash balances can exist and subsequently be eliminated, and a penalty loan will not be issued in FG; this would not be possible for a real company.

> **Example.**   A firm has $1,000,000 in cash at the beginning of a quarter and immediately spends $4,000,000 on capital investment, materials, and labor costs. If revenues collected at the end of the quarter are sufficient to offset the initial $3,000,000 cash deficit, a penalty loan will not be issued. Clearly, an actual firm is not able to carry large intra-period cash deficits.

Bankruptcy and Liquidation.   Unlike a real firm, an FG firm cannot go bankrupt. First, penalty loans will always be issued to forestall technical insolvency. Second, the common stock price will always remain positive. External funds can always be obtained by the issuance of common stock. This condition is not available for actual firms. They would be unable to find either lenders of funds or underwriters and investors in stock issues if the prospects for future restoration to profitability were very unlikely.

An FG firm can be liquidated. The conditions on plant, machinery, debt, and equity will have to be reviewed to determine the sequence of decisions necessary for liquidation.

> **Example.**   Due to dividend payout restrictions, debt and preferred stock must be retired before substantial liquidating dividends can be distributed. Other conditions require plant and machinery capacity to go to zero before other overhead and fixed selling and administrative costs cease.

The liquidation of an FG or actual company can be a sound decision if the long-run return from continuing the company is less than the return obtained from external investment of the net liquidation proceeds. The management must be quite certain that the declining firm performance is permanent and not due to a recession or short-run demand decrease.

Liquidation in the game is similar to that of a real firm. All assets either expire or can be converted to cash. After eliminating all other obligations, the remaining cash can be used for the distribution of common stock liquidating dividends. A manager must decide on the combination of stock repurchase and liquidating dividends to be used. In the game, at least one share of stock must remain outstanding even if all assets are distributed. The firm automatically retains one share even if an attempt is made for its retirement.

Taxes

The corporate income tax model used in the game is very much like an actual federal income tax. The major exception is that the game assumes an unlimited ability to recognize losses. In a real firm, if the income earned in the previous three years totals $3,000,000, a maximum income loss for tax purposes of $3,000,000 could be taken in the loss year. Any additional loss would be carried forward to be offset against positive taxable income in each of the next seven years. In the game, an automatic rebate equal to the tax rate times the quarterly loss is obtained in the quarter the loss occurs. Since a tax rebate will always partially offset a loss, the earnings loss used for income tax reduction is more favorable in FG than in an actual firm.

Equities

An FG company has a minimum common stock value in the $3.00 to $5.00 range, can always issue stock, and can't go bankrupt.

The conditions and rules that govern common and preferred stock in the game make them similar to actual securities. The business cycle and measures of risk of the firm are used in the preferred and common stock valuation models. The specific measures of risk with preferred and common stock are different.

Preferred Stock.   Preferred stock issuance is often avoided in financial decision making in the United States today. Based on current U.S. tax rules, it is most often a poor means of obtaining external funds. Interest on debt is tax deductible while preferred dividends have to be paid with after-corporate-tax dollars. Due to this, U.S. firms would prefer to use subordinated bonds, often convertible to equity, as a substitute for preferred stock issuance. Due to the tax disadvantage, the before-tax cost of preferred stock is substantially higher than low-rated subordinated debt. It is cost efficient to even issue "junk bonds" in lieu of preferred stock; the financial leverage effect for common stockholders is much lower per dollar of external funds received with using low-rated subordinated debt. Preferred stock issuance is often preferred to low-rated subordinated debt in England and other countries that allow the tax deductibility of preferred dividends. It is not a very useful source of additional financial leverage in the United States relative to debt financing, but it is included in the game to expose the participants to possible decision making in this area.

Preferred stock in a real situation is very similar to the stock included in the game. Most issues have a cumulative feature and are issued and repurchased using the same set of rules incorporated into the game. However, one condition is not realistic. In a real situation, the company's managers can decide to forgo preferred dividends even if bond indenture requirements are met. In the game, there is no control over preferred dividends. They are automatically paid or not paid depending on the debt and earnings position of the firm. The condition requiring adjusted operating income after financial expenses to exceed the before-tax cost of preferred dividends is quite restrictive. Dividend restriction covenants in real debt indentures as applied in FG are common. Often a bond indenture will specify a series of conditions that must be met before any distribution to equity holders is allowed. Specific hurdles are often required on a times-interest-earned ratio, a fixed-cost-coverage ratio, and a dividend-to-earnings payout rate. The amount of dividends that can be paid based on prior and current earnings is also a possible restriction. The restriction used in the game is intended to partially protect debt holders from companies providing cash flows to equity holders when earnings deteriorate.

Common Stock.   The manager can issue cash dividends and sell or repurchase stock. These three decisions give the manager control over the firm's common stock equity policies.

Dividends.   The cash dividend decision in the game is like the dividend decision in a real company. Dividends declared on a quarterly input sheet are paid in the same quarter. Since the game does not have specific shareholders and intra-quarter decisions are not made, a specific dividend declaration date, date of record, and payment date are not used.

Stock dividends, splits, and reverse splits are not available options. Options on stock dividends and splits have no value in FG since common stock value is not affected by the price level of a share. A condition where the marketability of a share decreases due to either very high or very low per-share dollar values is considered valid by many finance academicians and practitioners. The maintenance of a common stock trading range is achieved in the real world with stock dividends, splits, and reverse splits.

Stock Issuance.   Stock issuance in the game is in the form of a new "best effort" offering through an investment banker. The per-share offering price in the game closely duplicates the conditions of an actual share offering. The model includes several value-affecting components.

- The fixed- and variable-cost components cause the per share receipts to increase as the offering size increases. This results from a further spreading of the initial fixed cost over a larger number of shares.
- The security risk decreases as a function of a decrease in financial leverage. The decrease in security risk lowers the investors' required rate of return on common stock and contributes to higher prices for larger offerings.
- Expected earnings dilution from sharing future projects' NPVs with additional shareholders contributes to a smaller receipt per share. This occurs only if the market is inefficient in containing an unbiased estimate of the expected NPVs from the company's current and future investment projects.
- Price pressure exists if the market cannot easily absorb larger quantities of a security without share price decreases. The "imperfect substitute's hypothesis" can cause this condition, which results in lower proceeds per share as offer size increases.
- Signaling of new information by managers to shareholders can also occur with common stock offerings. Insiders, including managers, have more information about the future prospects of their firm than outside investors. Managers' decisions to issue securities may signal the future prospects of the company. Academic studies show a relationship between common stock offers and future company operating risk increases and lower than previously expected earnings. Given this information, it is not surprising that the average common stock price response to an equity-offer announcement is negative; shareholders lose wealth. This condition does not mean that managers should not issue these securities. The risk would increase or expected earnings would decrease in the future even if the stock issue did not occur. The issue is just a harbinger of future bad news. Thus, shareholders' wealth would probably still decrease, but just not as soon.
- Agency costs for external issues of debt and equity could cause the cost of funds to increase still further for larger-sized issues. Agency costs arise when investors underestimate the true value of the firm because of both incomplete information and an expectation that the insider, in this case the manager, will transfer wealth away from them.

Example.   An analogy to this phenomenon is with the sale of a used car. The buyer wants a quality car in good operating condition that will need minimal repairs. The buyer also knows that the seller must be selling the car for a reason, the expectation of large future repairs being one possible motivation for the sale. The buyer is at a disadvantage because the seller has asymmetric (insider) information about the car's quality. Due to this potential for getting a "lemon," the buyer is only willing to give a low bid. The bid would be lower than the bid on an average car due to the likelihood that the car for sale is below average quality—otherwise it would not be for sale. The same phenomenon holds with security issues. If a manager, operating in the wealth-maximizing interest of current stockholders, is selling securities, they are likely to be a "lemon" and be overvalued. The outside investor then marks down the bid to reflect the likelihood that the security is overvalued. If the car or security seller could guarantee the quality of the offer, the underbidding would not occur.

All of the above conditions are likely to affect the discount from current common share price required to sell new shares. They can all be viewed to affect the issue share price discount used in FG.

In an actual issuance, managers may specify a minimum price they are willing to accept. This permits the company and the investment banker to terminate the planned issuance if market conditions are too poor. Managers in the game do not have this option. The investment banker will market the entire issue at a market-determined price. The FG company does not have the opportunity to set an offering price range based on the demand for the securities offered.

Stock Repurchase.   Stock repurchase in FG is initiated through a tender offer. The manager specifies both an offering price and the number of shares tendered. The fees and transaction costs of a successful tender are covered by the spread between the tender price and the current stock price at the time of the decision input. Also, the spread is directly related to the percentage of the outstanding stock tendered. This premium will be higher when part of the original 1,000,000 shares is being tendered. Shares issued since quarter 1 require a smaller spread.

In an actual situation as in FG, longer-term security holders often require higher-priced premiums before selling than do more recent stockholders. A tender by management can signal a revision of investor expectations and pressure for higher share prices. The premium is also affected by the per-share dollar value. The price volatility of lower-priced stocks is greater—generally because such firms' future earning potential is more uncertain. To have a successful tender, a higher markup is necessary with the lower-priced stock.

A tender in the game is automatically exercised by management if less than the total number of originally desired shares is tendered. In an actual situation, the manager has the option to refuse repurchase of shares if the entire number of shares desired is not tendered. Additionally, real-world managers have an option to extend the tender date or modify the tender offer if the desired number of shares are not tendered. Alternatively, the FG manager can issue a revised tender offer every quarter.

Valuation.   The stock valuation model is sufficiently complex, as in a real situation, to prohibit the manager from determining its exact nature. The game purposely does not define the common stock valuation model. Through testing and analysis, managers can assess the importance and possibly determine the effect of changes in the variables that affect common stock price. The inability to understand the model arises from the interdependence of many variables, including:

1. Historical and projected earnings per share.
2. Anticipated earnings per share growth.
3. The economic environment.
4. Uncertainty of future earnings.
5. The dividend payout.
6. The stability of the dividends.

Example.   The positive effect of an increase in earnings per share can be less than the negative effect of concurrent changes in (1) the economic environment, (2) the uncertainty of future earnings, and (3) both the stability and payout of dividends. Thus, a decrease in share price can occur even though the earnings per share are increasing. This is commonly found in actual stock price movements. In a second example, the price of the stock will increase if earnings per share sustain a higher growth rate than has been obtained historically, earnings' uncertainty decreases, or a proper shift in the dividend payout and stability policy is achieved.

The variables incorporated into the game's common stock valuation model are the ones that investment services and investors have historically stated they use in determining the value of a company. Here are four common factors:

- Historical earnings and earnings growth trends are used in estimating the future earnings, dividends, and price appreciation of a company's common stock. The use of earnings growth trends in the valuation model reduces the effects of temporary or short-run conditions on the share prices.
- Uncertainty affects shareholders' valuation of shares. Uncertainty implies a greater risk of not obtaining the expected earnings and earnings growth rate. The firm with a less certain future would have to offer higher expected returns to command the same share price. In the game, a firm that maintains a stable earnings and earnings growth is viewed as having a more certain future than a firm with a more volatile or erratic history.
- The general level of business activity and inflation affect the market's valuation of all equities and thus should impact a given company's stock price. This condition is consistent with research indicating that most share price changes are closely correlated to a general market index.
- Dividend policy also affects valuation. A following section on dividend yield discusses dividend policy more completely.

The variables included in the FG valuation model provide share price and share price movements somewhat similar to those found in current markets. Again, emphasis in the game is on forming a valuation model that differentiates between varying levels of performance. A partial loss of realism holds.

Short-Term Share Value.   Share price changes required for a tender or stock offering are only temporary and do not directly affect the quarter's ending price. The tender or issuance can indirectly affect prices through the valuation conditions just outlined. The issuance and tender result in short-term supply and demand shifts that cause the stock price to vary from its long-run underlying value. The quarterly ending price assumes a restoration to the long-run supply and demand equilibrium and the stock's true long-run value. Evidence is consistent with short-term price pressure existing on stock issuance and purchase in the real world.

The numerous rules and conditions that govern FG common stock are fairly complex, enabling stock prices to behave much like securities in public trading. Decision alternatives available to the game participant closely duplicate the alternatives available to an operating manager.

Performance Information

The performance measures provided quarterly in the game are to be used to assess a manager's effectiveness in operating the company. Most measures generated in the game are commonly found and used in the evaluation of actual companies.

Multiple performance measures should be used as a set in evaluating performance.

The performance measures should be used as an integrated set. Different types of period-to-period variations can temporarily distort specific measures. By viewing the measures collectively, the manager can determine whether systematic shifts of several measures are occurring and why specific measures are changing. This analysis should be used to verify the consistency of actual results with the firm's objectives and, if they are not consistent, to determine what corrective actions are appropriate. To be successful, the manager in an FG firm must perform the same type of analysis required in an actual company. Greater uncertainty arising from less reliable performance measures makes the actual manager's task more difficult.

As in an actual company, a manager's performance should be measured relative to other companies' performance and relative to the historical position of the firm. An absolute measure has little real meaning either in the game or in an actual firm.

> **Example.**   A firm that maintains 10 percent compounded growth in accumulated wealth performs poorly if all other firms obtain 20 percent. Alternatively, a 10 percent growth rate might be excellent performance if the next-best firm obtains a 5 percent rate. If a business recession is used in FG, the highest-performing company may still have a material loss of wealth. Superior management skills would be demonstrated if this company outperformed the other firms by having the smallest losses and having shareholders with the greatest accumulated wealth per share at the end of the game.

A manager often has difficulty disregarding preconceived notions of appropriate performance. This can have negative effects on attitudes, analysis, the formulated company plan, and future performance. The FG manager should maintain objectivity by judging the firm's performance relative to other firms, not by an arbitrary rule of thumb from outside the game. This same objective approach is appropriate for use in managing a real company.

The stability of the more reliable performance measures increases as game play progresses. Initially, a firm might be ranked first in accumulated wealth and in the next quarter be ranked last. If firms are operating in a fairly stable economy, changes in ranking among firms over time will be both less dramatic and less frequent. This is especially true with accumulated wealth. Conversely, a more unstable business environment increases the likelihood of more random rank changes. The largest daily stock price changes indicate this condition is fairly realistic; it can be frustrating to the competent manager when the company's stock price does not appear to consistently reflect its high performance measures.

The specific performance measures incorporated into the summary sheet and the overall performance report each quarter are now examined. For many reasons noted in the following sections, the measures are potentially more reliable in the game than in the evaluation of actual firms.

Accumulated Wealth.   Accumulated wealth is a hybrid performance measure developed for use in the game. At the start of the game, all companies have the same share price. Managers' decisions affect both stock price and dividend payout, which are the two items of information needed to calculate accumulated wealth. Management decisions and environment conditions determine this performance measure.

Stock price is the major item that affects the accumulated wealth measure early in the game since there are no initial accumulated dividends or investment returns on previous dividends. The quarterly cash dividends accumulate and have an increasing effect as the simulation progresses through successive iterations. This effect is increased by the quarterly compounded earnings rate applied to all previously paid-out dividends in deriving the accumulated wealth measure. Since accumulated wealth is dominated by share price earlier in the game, its stability is almost completely dependent on the volatility of the share price. Shifts in company ranking with accumulated wealth can be both frequent and large. As accumulated dividends and earnings on previous dividends increase, and as the company builds its long-term performance (good or bad) the accumulated wealth measure gains stability and reliability.

The major cause of the measure's instability is short-term stock price changes, which can vary from the long-run trend for price changes. Even unsound decisions can have temporary effects on stock prices and the accumulated wealth figure.

Example.   Instability could be caused by excess production. If a firm overproduces, the per-unit production cost for the period can often be decreased. Spreading the fixed costs over a larger number of units causes this to occur. With a lower cost per unit matched against revenues, the firm can have higher earnings in the quarter than it would have obtained with lower production levels. The larger ending inventory then carries a larger proportion of the current period's fixed costs to the next period. Temporarily, earnings per share and the earnings-per-share growth rate are favorably affected and a greater positive change in stock prices might be gained. The long-term effect might be negative since the fixed costs in the higher inventory eventually end up negatively affecting earnings in the future period when the inventory is reduced. Astute informed investors would likely decrease the stock value of the company when the inventory expansion occurred; naïve investors might falsely bid the share price in the first period and then bid it down when the true impact of the event is found in a later period. In FG, investors are more naïve than in the real world. Security markets in the real world are more efficient in incorporating the long-term effects of a management outcome, like the inventory overstocking. There, analysts specializing in evaluating a small number of industry-related stocks would spot the excess inventory problem and project the consequences of this problem on current and future earning using pro forma statements similar to the ones used in FG.

The manager is cautioned against accepting accumulated wealth or any other single measure in judging the overall performance of the companies in the game. In the example just covered, the inventory buildup should have warned the management of a possible temporary upward bias in accumulated wealth. An examination of the other measures and the contents of the financial statements should be made by the managers to disclose impending permanent future changes in accumulated wealth.

Example (continued).   The pro forma planning for the next period of play that appropriately brings the company's inventory back to its optimal safety-stock level would capture the negative earnings impact from the excess inventory problem of the current period. This process is followed by many actual companies that provide new or revised earnings per share (EPS) estimates for the next period when they announce their current earnings. If the manager had a reasonable valuation model, like the one that the above analyst would use, the stock price correction that would likely occur now due to the impact of excess inventory on current and future earnings would also be estimated for internal planning purposes, including a possible revision in expected future cash flows and the company's WACC.

Accumulated wealth measures provide the same information used by actual investors in determining their return on investment. Appreciation or depreciation of a share's price plus dividends is divided by the initial investment per share to give a percent gain or loss from the investment. Since all FG companies start with the same price per share, or initial investment, there is no need to divide this into the gains or losses in obtaining a number to compare the relative position. Furthermore, a dollar of cash dividend in quarter 1 must be worth more than a dollar of cash dividend in quarter 15 because the investor can invest the first dollar and obtain compounded interest and/or appreciation for 14 quarters.

To recognize the opportunity return available to investors, accumulated wealth each period is adjusted by multiplying previously distributed dividends by the yield on risk-free marketable securities that is adjusted upward by a 1.5 percent premium. The marketable security rate plus 1.5 percent is an after-tax return to the investor and is an implied opportunity rate of return available to investors. This rate is a risk-free after-tax opportunity cost that can be used by management in judging whether they are efficiently utilizing funds not needed for efficient operation of the firm. Internal funds that do not earn at least the risk-adjusted equivalent to the external opportunity rate should be returned to investors by retirement of debt, repurchase of equities, or payment of extra dividends to common stockholders. Either excess retention or excess distributions would result in a lower accumulated wealth figure.

The accumulated wealth figure provides a useful measure of the manager's ability to operate in the wealth-maximizing interest of the common shareholder. It is also the best single measure of a company's performance in the game.

Quarterly Earnings.   The quarterly earnings per share (EPS) is a short-run performance measure. It is weak as an overall measure of performance for several reasons:

- Many of the valuation factors discussed previously are not incorporated in EPS.
- The current EPS change can be in the opposite direction from the true change in long-term shareholder wealth.

Example.   In an expanding economy, an excessive increase in financial leverage will immediately increase EPS. The current EPS change does not reflect the increased risk resulting from excessive financial leverage. This increased risk might more than offset the higher temporary EPS.

- Due to the heavy operating leverage of an FG firm, the EPS is quite unstable. It can vary significantly with changes in the business cycle.
- EPS is subject to substantial management manipulation. EPS levels and stability can be affected by period-to-period shifts in production levels and discretionary management-controlled costs.

These four reasons make EPS an unreliable performance measure even though some added information might be obtained by using it with other performance measures. The use of EPS as a performance measure in the real world suffers from the same weaknesses found in the game.

Dividend Yield.   Dividends are a very important valuation component for mature or low-growth firms. Dividend yields can be used as an appropriate performance measure for firms that have low expected rates of growth. An increasing yield induced by a price decrease would indicate either a general market shift in required long-term return rates or a specific negative shift in shareholders' evaluation of the value of the firm that may be either short term or long term. The second condition should initiate management analysis to determine what has caused the shift and if the cause represents a long-term phenomenon.

The reliability of dividend yield as a performance measure decreases as the importance of dividends decreases or as price volatility increases. The importance of dividends is inversely related to the earnings growth rate of a firm. Therefore, a high-growth firm could be operating counter to the wealth-maximizing interests of its shareholders if it distributes cash in dividends. The dividends could possibly earn more if retained by the firm than if distributed to investors. In this case, a dividend yield will be inversely related to shareholder wealth and will not be a valid measure of performance.

As price volatility increases, there is a direct increase in the volatility of the dividend yield performance measure, assuming dividends remain stable. Comparability is lost if the rate and direction of the shift in prices are not the same each period for all companies being evaluated. This condition occurs frequently in the game and in the real world. A secondary problem occurs if, with volatile prices, the manager attempts to maintain a constant dividend yield. Both a loss in dividend stability and a volatile dividend payout will result. Since valuation is affected by both items, the maximization of common stockholder wealth can be substantially reduced. This type of problem is common when a manager attempts to focus too much attention on the maintenance or enhancement of a given performance measure without considering the underlying policies being affected.

Price-Earnings (P/E) Ratio.   The P/E ratio is commonly used by investors as an indicator of the "quality" of a company's current earnings. Investors are willing to pay higher ratios for higher-quality earnings. The variables used in the game's valuation of common stock more rigorously define the rather vague term *quality* used by investors. Current EPS, projected EPS, expected growth, and expected certainty of future earnings are the key earnings factors that affect valuation. Investors' expectations concerning these factors are mainly formed from historical evidence of earnings growth and the stability of the growth. The game duplicates this type of environment.

The ability to compare the P/E ratios of different firms and the reliability of this ratio are both suspect. The problems come from the two components—price and earnings—used in the definition of the P/E ratio. The earnings per share used in the denominator of the ratio has several weaknesses just covered in the "Quarterly Earnings" section. The weaknesses result in earnings figures that cannot be reliably used in determining long-run performance. Additionally, price volatility decreases the stability of the ratio through time, which further lessens the reliability of the quarterly P/E ratio. Though it is probably better than dividend yield as a performance measure, the P/E ratio still has many weaknesses that restrain a manager from placing much confidence in it whether in the game or in the actual analysis of companies.

Return on Investment and Return on Equity. Return on investment (ROI equals earnings/assets) and return on equity (ROE equals earnings/equity) measures are commonly used in evaluating the performance of divisions, product areas, and entire companies. Several weaknesses restrict their value as successful measures of performance.

- The inclusion of the expected future earnings stream is avoided since only current earnings are used. Investors will be more concerned with the firm's future prospects for generating funds since their wealth maximization comes from maximizing future earnings on their invested capital.
- Both ROI and ROE include the weaknesses found in using quarterly earnings as a measure of performance described earlier. This occurs since earnings are used in the numerators of both ROI and ROE.
- The ROI and ROE performance measures also do not incorporate any measure of risk or uncertainty. For comparability between firms, ROI and ROE figures are not modified to reflect either the stability or the reliability of future earnings.
- Problems also arise in the denominator. Particularly in a real situation, the investment bases of the different firms are often not comparable. This arises from inappropriately using historical costs or adjusted historical costs in measuring total investment.

Example.   If net assets (original cost less accumulated depreciation) are used, a new facility with larger amounts of undepreciated new equipment would have a much larger investment base than an older firm with almost completely depreciated facilities. In this case, the new facility's ROI and ROE could be substantially below those of the older plant, not because of differences in management performance but because of differences in the life of the equipment. Alternatively, if gross assets or original costs were used in the definition of ROI and ROE, the older facility's performance measure could be unrealistically low due to the technological disadvantage of the old as opposed to the new facility.

ROI and ROE generally are more reliable performance measures in the game than in an operating environment. The investment or asset base of ROI and ROE is initially the same for all firms in FG. Since equipment replacement and heavy capital acquisitions are required in approximately the same time pattern, major divergences in average asset life and therefore in net asset value are uncommon even after several quarters. Distortions in comparability can occur if the quantity and type of capital budgeting additions vary materially. Distortions may be caused by major differences in total investment and different patterns of cash flows that result from different selections. Furthermore, the firms in FG are in the same industry and have the same business risks and relative earnings instability. Thus, ROE and ROI can provide the FG manager with additional partially reliable information for assessing performance—information often not available with an actual company.

Review of Performance Measures.   The performance measures just reviewed are all commonly found and widely used in actual companies. In both FG and an actual company, the set of performance measures is used by management in assessing the relative performance of the company both over time and in comparison to other companies. An analysis of the financial statements and additional summary data are also required for estimating the firm's historical performance and its prospects for continued achievement of performance goals. Along with comparing performance, the above measures can signal to managers that their previous decisions or strategies might need revision.

Extraordinary Items, Fires, and Strikes

Increased uncertainties and new decision situations are faced by the manager when the instructor initiates any of these options: extraordinary items, a fire, or a labor strike. Extraordinary losses charged in the game have the same effects that expropriation, embezzlement, default, or one of many other windfall loss events may have on the financial statements, performance measures, and management decision requirements of an actual firm. A positive extraordinary gain has the same effect as a favorable lawsuit settlement or a windfall gain on the sale of assets.

The fire is less realistic. First, it would take a busy arsonist to strike all firms in the same quarter. Second, if this did occur, we would also expect many changes in future unit demand and prices due to shortages. There are no carry-forward effects of this nature. Third, only inventory and machinery are affected. The plant that contains these items remains undamaged. This unrealistic condition was incorporated so that production limitations would last only the one quarter needed to rebuild machinery.

The strike contains probability estimates and costs not normally available or determinable in an actual strike situation. In the game, this reduces the strike problem to one of risk rather than uncertainty, and it enables currently available solution techniques to be used in making a decision. Strikes also have an indeterminate life, which adds to the manager's risk. In FG, only a one-period strike occurs unless the instructor initiates multiple contiguous-period strikes.

Conclusion

Most of the definitions, analytical tools, and solution techniques learned in game play are transferable to the real world. Many specific rules and conditions found in the actual environment are not included in FG. By recognizing why and how decisions are different, managers can greatly enhance their ability to transfer knowledge gained from game play to analysis and decision making in an actual company.

Index

A

Abandonment decision, 30
Accelerated depreciation, 101
Account information, 13
Account settings, 12–13
Accounts payable, 63
Accounts receivable, 28–29, 97–98
Accumulated wealth, 19–20, 79–80, 113–114
    wealth maximization, 3, 7, 20, 45
Administrative expenses; *see* Selling and administrative
    expenses
Advance code, 10
Advertising, 34, 63–64, 82, 101
Agency cost of equity, 37, 109
Average costing, 63
Average unit production cost, 63

B

Back-ordering, 97
Bankruptcy, 107
Basic account information, 13
Best effort offering, 109
Bond call, 71
Bond financing, 26
Bond maturity, 71
Bond redemption costs, 70
Bond retirement, 105
Book value, 74
Budgeted financial statements; *see* Pro forma financial
    statements
Building block approach, 21
Business cycle, debt costs and, 102–103
Business risk, 92

C

Call premium, 26, 104–105
Callable bonds, 105
Capacity limits, 33
Capital budgeting analysis, 24–25
Capital budgeting decisions, 35

Capital budgeting projects, 30, 56, 60–63, 82, 101
    accounting impacts, 62
    manager objective, 62
    rules for, 60–61
Capital structure, 25–27, 100
    optimal structure, 25
    weighted average cost of capital and, 25–26
Carrying costs, 23, 29
Cash balance, 23
Cash flows
    intra-quarter cash flows, 107
    product sales and, 82, 97–98
Cash inflows, 50, 67–68
Cash and liquidity management, 23–24, 27, 35, 52–55
    cash shortages, 53–55, 82
    marketable securities liquidation, 53–54, 82
    short-term investments, 52–53
    short-term penalty loans, 54–55
Cash outflow, 56–60, 62, 64, 67, 69–70
Cash shortages, 53–55, 82
    accounting impacts, 54–55
    manager objectives, 54–55
    marketable securities liquidation, 53
    short-term penalty loans, 53
Cash throw-off, 38
Chief executive officer (CEO), 1
Chief financial officer (CFO), 1
Chief operating officer (COO), 1
Common stock, 75–79, 82–83, 108
    accounting impacts, 76, 78
    cost of, 26
    dividends, 28, 78–79, 83, 109; *see also* Dividend(s)
    issuance of, 76–77, 109–110
    manager objective, 75, 77
    new issues, 83
    repurchase of, 77–78, 83, 110
    shareholders wealth maximization, 3
    short-term share value, 111–112
    tender offer, 83
    valuation of, 75, 82, 110–111
Common tender price, 77

Common tender of sell/share, 76
Company account, 11
Company environment, 45
    risk bearing in, 39–41
Company growth opportunities, 27
Company life cycle, 37–39
    declining companies, 38
    impacts on strategy, 37–39
    mature companies, 38
    new companies, 37–38
Company management instructions, 43–45
Company name, 13
Company operating decisions, 15
Company operating rules, 45–47
    industry environment, 45–46
    operation of the company, 46–47
Company strategy
    approach to, 22
    need for, 20–21
Computer requirements, 9
Contribution margin, 33
Cost of capital, 25–27, 29, 35
Cost of goods sold, 58
Credit policy, 28
Cumulative performance, 5
Current company quarter, 11

D

Debt costs, 66–71, 83
    business cycle and, 102–103
    maturity and, 102
Debt financing, 26; *see also* Loans and debt costs
    intermediate-term loans, 68–69, 104
    long-term bonds, 70–71
    short-term loans, 67–68
    short-term penalty loans, 68
    similarities/differences, 106
Debt indentures, 28, 74, 93
Debt interest coverage ratios, 29
Debt-to-equity ratio, 25
Decisions, 5, 94–95
    company management instructions, 43–44
    integrating set of, 35–37
    interrelationship among, 21
    requirements for, 94–95
    secondary effects of, 6
Declining companies, 38
Deferred income taxes payable, 101
Demand and demand elasticity, 30, 33–34, 98
Demand estimates/forecasts, 49–50, 86
    purchase of, 49, 87
Depreciable life, 100
Depreciation, 58–59, 62
Direct labor, 56–57, 60, 82–83
Discount policy, 28, 51–52
Discount on receivables, 28–29
Dividend(s), 83, 109
    common stock dividends, 78–79, 83
    dividend policy, 27–28, 40
    payout rate, 27, 75
    preferred stock and, 72–73, 86
Dividend stability, 8, 27–29, 75
Dividend yield, 80
    as performance measure, 115

E

E-mail address, 13
Earnings dilution, 109
Earnings per share (EPS), 75, 80
    as performance measure, 114–115
Economic conditions, 7, 66, 75
Economic order quantity (EOQ), 8, 23–24, 29–30, 105
Economies of scale, 31
Edit decisions, 12, 16
Ending inventory, 63
Equities, 72–79, 108–112; *see also* Common stock
    preferred stock, 72–74, 108
Excess free cash flow problem, 38
External financing, 35
Extraordinary items, 64–66, 117
    extraordinary loss or gain, 65, 83
    fire, 65–66, 117
    labor strike, 64–65, 117

F

Financial expenses, 29, 102
Financial leverage, 8, 40, 67
    constraints on, 93
Financial leverage ratios, 29
Financial statement accounts
    advertising, 101
    equities, 108–112
    extraordinary items, fires, and strikes, 117
    financial expenses, 102–107
    performance information, 112–117
    production costs, 99–101
    revenues, 96–99
    selling and administrative expenses, 101
    taxes, 107–108
Financial statement construction, 8
Financing decisions, 15
FinGame (FG); *see also* Game environment
    as comprehensive case study, 6
    computer requirements, 9
    general conditions, 89
    getting a company account, 11
    initial instructions, 10
    interdisciplinary approach and, 6
    main menu options, 11, 13–14
    managers' risk tolerance in, 40–41
    as multiple-period decision problem, 5
    as noninteractive, 5
    objective of, 2
    operating instructions, 11–12
    overview of, 1–2
    plan of attack for, 21–37
    preparation requirements, 7–8
    purpose of game, 2
    quick reference source, 82–88
    real world vs. game environment, 89–91
    simple models, 89–90
    text contents, 2–3
    uncertainty in, 91–93
    underlying simulation, 16–17
    web access and use, 9–17
Fire, 59n, 65–66, 84, 117
Firm size, 96
Fixed costs, 62
Fixed flotation fee, 105–106

Fixed production expenses, 62
Flexibility, constraints on, 94
Flexible budgeting, 23
Flotation cost, 104
Forced liquidation of marketable securities/short-term
    investments, 53, 84
Forecast reliability, 35, 92
Funds of last resort, 106
Future level of earnings, 75

G

Game environment, 3–7
    financial leverage, 93
    informal organizational structure, 95–96
    initial instructions, 10
    operating leverage and, 92–93
    operating procedures for, 4, 11–12
    real world vs., 89–91
    size of firm, 96
    steps in, 44–45
    uncertainty and, 91–93
Generally Accepted Accounting Principles
    (GAAP), 101
Going concern value, 38
Going-concern-versus-abandonment decision, 30
Group code, 11
Growth rate of earnings, 75

I

Imperfect substitutes hypothesis, 109
Income, 47
Indentures, 28, 74, 93
Indirect labor costs, 62
Industry environment, 45–46
Inflation, 66
Informal organizational structure, 95–96
Information, 23, 49
Initializing starting company, 10
Insolvency risk, 66, 103
Interest rates, 66
    factors determining, 66–67
Intermediate-term loans, 68–69, 84, 104
    accounting impacts of, 69
    rules of, 68–69
Internet access; *see* Web access and use
Interpersonal interaction, 95
Intra-quarter cash flows, 107
Inventory, 29–30, 34, 40, 50
    carrying costs of, 29
    ending inventory, 63

J

Join a group entry code, 10, 12
Junk bonds, 108

L

Labor costs, 61, 65, 99
Labor savings, 61
Labor strike, 64–65, 84
Large and small businesses, 96
Lead-time requirements, 100
Lease/rent, 62
Life cycle; *see* Company life cycle

Liquidation, 38–39, 82, 107
Liquidation fee, 54
Liquidity, 35
Liquidity management; *see* Cash and liquidity
    management
Loans and debt costs, 66–71
    intermediate-term loans, 68–69, 84
    long-term bonds, 26, 70–71, 84
    short-term loans, 67–68, 88
    short-term penalty loans, 54–55, 68, 88
Locked-out position, 6
Logging onto FinGame site, 11
Logout, 12
Long-term bonds, 26, 70–71, 84, 104
    accounting impacts, 71
    rules of, 70
Long-term planning, 94–95

M

Machine and plant capacity, 29–30
Machinery, 58–60, 84–85, 100–101
    accounting impacts, 59–60
    capacity and depreciation of, 59
    excess machinery, 59
    manager objective, 60
    one-period delay in, 59
Main menu options, 11, 13–14
    add a view group, 14
    basic account information, 13
    change user name, 13
    change password, 13
    enabling other features, 13–14
    supplemental materials, 14
    view other companies, 13–14
Management plan
    advertising, 34
    capital budgeting analysis, 24–25
    capital structure and WACC, 25–27
    cash and liquidity management, 23–24
    discount on receivables, 28–29
    dividend policy, 27–28
    establishing of, 19–20
    need for company strategy, 20–21
    overview of strategy, 19–20
    possible planning approach, 22
    pro forma statements, 22–23
    production strategy, 29–30
    unit pricing strategy, 30–34
Managers and managers' decisions, 1, 4
    financial leverage, 93
    integrating decision set, 35–37
    life cycle impacts, 37–39
    middle-of-the-road managers, 40
    performance of, 20
    product pricing, control of, 51, 86
    risk-averse managers, 39–40, 93
    risk-bearing tolerance, 39–41
    risk-taking managers, 39
    uncertain environment and, 6, 92
Marginal return on investment, 33
Marketable securities, 23, 35, 85, 98–99
    liquidation of, 53–54, 82, 84–85
    yield, 52–53
Marketing and sales, real world vs., 97

Materials, 56, 85, 99
Mature companies, 38
Maturity (of debt issues), 102
Maximizing shareholder wealth, 3, 7
Micromanaging, 20
Middle-of-the-road managers, 40

N

Negative cash balances, 107
Negative-growth industries, 38
Net present value (NPV), 24–25, 27, 35, 38, 101
New companies, 37–38
New investment decisions, 15
New issues, 83
Noninteractive environment, 5
Nonspecific environment, 5

O

Offering premium, 66
Operating instructions; *see* Game environment
Operating leverage, 8, 92–93
Operation of the company, 46–47
Opportunity cost, 28
Optimal decisions, 6, 23
Overhead/other overhead costs, 60, 62–63, 82, 85, 99
Overleveraged capital structure, 104–105

P

Password, 13
    changing password, 13
Payout rate, 27
Penalty loans, 23, 54, 82, 85, 106
Percentage-of-completion loans, 100
Performance information, 79–81
    accumulated wealth, 79–80, 113–114
    dividend yield, 80, 115
    earnings per share (EPS), 114–115
    price-earnings ratio, 80, 115
    quarterly earnings, 80, 114–115
    return on equity (ROE), 81, 116
    return on investment (ROI), 80–81, 116
    review of, 116–117
Performance Report, 4, 46, 58
Perpetual security, 53, 72
Planning approach, 3, 22; *see also* Management plan
Plant, 57–58, 85
    accounting impacts, 58
    depreciation of, 58
Plant capacity, 29–30
Plant costs, 100–101
Position Statement, 4, 46–47
Preferred stock, 72–74, 86, 108
    accounting impacts, 72–73
    cost of, 26
    dividend payment restrictions, 28, 72–73
    issuance of, 73–74
    repurchases of, 74
Price-demand relationships, 33
Price-earnings (P/E) ratio, 80, 115
Price forecasts, 49, 87
Pricing strategy
    optimal manager-determined price, 33
    possible method of attack, 33–34

price increases, 32–33
price reductions, 31
suboptimal/second-best policy, 32–33
uncertainty and, 92
unit pricing strategy, 30–34
Prime rate, 103
Pro forma (budgeted) financial statements, 9, 35
    need for, 22–23
Pro forma decision inputs, 14–16
Pro Forma decision sheet, 14, 44
Pro forma simulation, 12
Product demanded and sold, 50–51, 86
    accounting impacts, 51
    manager objective, 51–52
    rules for, 51
    uncertainty and, 91–92
    unit production, 51
Product price, demand estimates and, 86
Product sales, 96–97
Product sales estimation, 47–49, 82, 97
Product selling price per unit, manager-controlled, 51, 86
Product sold (cash flows), 86
Product sold (units and sales revenue), 86
Product unit production, 87
Production costs, 55–63, 87, 99–101
    capital budgeting projects, 60–62
    direct labor, 56–57, 99
    machinery, 58–60
    materials, 56, 99
    other overhead, 62–63, 99
    plant, 57–58
    summary on, 63
    warehouse fees, 57, 99–100
Production line improvements, 61
Production strategy, 29–30
    inventory, 29
    machine and plant capacity, 29–30
Profit contribution, 29
Profit margin, 32
Property taxes, 62
Public offering, 106
Purchase of demand and price forecast, 49–50, 87
    accounting impacts, 49
    manager objective, 50
Pure play approach, 26

Q

Quality of earnings, 115
Quarterly company simulations
    edit actual decision inputs, 16
    edit pro forma decision inputs, 14–16
    process for, 14–17
    run actual simulation, 16
Quarterly earnings (quarterly EPS), 80, 114–115
Quarterly Performance Report, 46

R

Reactive role, 20
Real-world models, 90
Receivables, 28, 52, 87
Registration key code, 11
Repurchase of common/preferred stock, 74, 77–78, 83, 110
Retirement decision, 69–70

Retirement of principal, 105
Return on equity (ROE), 81
    as performance measure, 116
Return on investment (ROI), 33
    as performance measure, 80–81, 116
Revenues, 47–52, 96–99
    manager control of product pricing, 51
    manager objective, 49
    product demanded and sold, 50–51
    product sales/sales estimation, 47–49, 96–97
    purchase of demand and price forecast, 49
    sales discounts, 51–52
Reverse stock splits, 109
Risk
    business risk, 92
    cost of capital and, 25–27, 29, 35
    insolvency risk, 66, 103
    short-term investments, 52–53
Risk-adjusted discount (RAD) rate, 26, 28
Risk-averse managers, 27, 39–40, 93
Risk-bearing tolerance of managers, 39–41
Risk of insolvency, 66, 103
Risk premiums, 75
Risk-taking managers, 39
Run simulation, 16

S
Safety-stock, 29
Sales discounts, 51–52, 87, 97–98
Salvage value, 58
Securities and Exchange Commission (SEC), 13
Selling and administrative expenses, 63–64, 87, 101
    accounting impacts, 64
    advertising costs, 64, 101
    conditions of, 63
    manager objective, 64
Serial bonds, 106
Short-term investments, 35, 47, 52–53, 87
    accounting impacts, 52–53
    liquidation of, 84
    manager objective, 53
    risk level of, 52–53
Short-term loan rate, 28
Short-term loans, 67–68, 88, 103–104
Short-term penalty loans, 54–55, 68, 88, 106
Short-term share value, 111–112
Signaling of new information, 109
Simple models, 89–90
Single-stage production, 100
Size-of-offering premium, 103
Small businesses, 96, 107
Stability of dividends, 8, 27–29, 75
Stock issuance, 76–77, 109–110
Stock-out costs, 23, 29, 31, 34
Stock-out models, 8
Stock repurchases, 74, 110
Stock splits, 109

Stock valuation model, 110–111
Straight-line depreciation, 59, 101
Strategy, defined, 20; *see also* Management plan
Strike, 64–65, 84, 117
Strike settlement decision, 65
Summary data, 4, 48
Summary Sheet, 46, 59, 61
Supplemental materials, 14

T
Tax rebate, 108
Taxes, 71, 88, 100, 107–108
Teams, 95
10Q (quarterly) statements, 13–14
Tender offer, 77–78, 83, 110
Term debt, 104
Theoretically sound models, 90–91
Thin-market conditions, 99
Treasury bills, 53

U
Uncertainty, game environment and, 6, 91–93
    financial leverage and, 93
    future demand and price, 92
    operating leverage, 92–93
    producing unknown product, 91
Underlying simulation, 16–17
Underlying yield curve, 66
Unit price of product, 51
Unit pricing strategy, 30–34
Unit production, 51
Unit sales/sales price, 28–30
Useful life, 100
User name, 13
    changing name, 13

V
Valuation of common stock, 75
View group/group code, 14
View other companies, 13–14
View results, 12; *see also* Game environment

W
Warehouse fees, 29, 57, 88, 99–100
Wealth, 19
Wealth maximization, 3, 7, 20, 45
Web access and use, 9–17
    login and password, 11
Weighted average cost of capital (WACC), 25–28, 38
    capital structure and, 25–26

Y
Yield curve, 66, 102
    negative slope of, 102